City
ON A
Hill

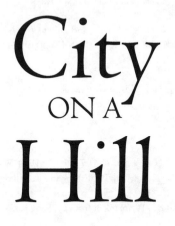

City
ON A
Hill

Reclaiming the Biblical Pattern
for the Church in the 21st Century

PHILIP GRAHAM RYKEN

MOODY PUBLISHERS
CHICAGO

All Scripture quotations, unless otherwise indicated, are taken from the *Holy Bible, New International Version*®. NIV®. Copyright © 1973, 1978, 1984 by International Bible Society. Used by permission of Zondervan Publishing House. All rights reserved.

Scripture quotations marked KJV are taken from the King James Version.

Scripture quotations marked TLB are taken from *The Living Bible* copyright © 1971. Used by permission of Tyndale House Publishers, Inc., Wheaton, Illinois 60189. All rights reserved.

Library of Congress Cataloging-in-Publication Data

Ryken, Philip Graham, 1966-
    City on a hill : reclaiming the biblical pattern for the church in the 21st century/
Philip Graham Ryken.
        p. cm.
    Includes bibliographical references.
    ISBN 0-8024-4199-8
    I. Church. 2. Church—Biblical teaching. 3. Christianity—United States. I. Title.

BV600.3 .R95 2003
262'.001'7—dc21

2002152178

ISBN: 0-8024-4199-8

1 3 5 7 9 10 8 6 4 2

Printed in the United States of America

A city on a hill cannot be hidden.
(Matthew 5:14)

Dedicated to four mentors in ministry:

the late Rev. Robert Harvey
of Bethel Orthodox Presbyterian Church in Wheaton, Illinois;

the Rev. George R. Cottenden
of Trinity Orthodox Presbyterian Church in Hatboro, Pennsylvania;

the late Rev. William Still
of Gilcomston South Church in Aberdeen, Scotland;

and the Rev. D. Marion Clark,
formerly of Tenth Presbyterian Church in Philadelphia
and now of Faith Presbyterian Church in Gainesville, Florida.

In his own way, each of these good men
shaped my understanding of theology and ministry,
helping me understand what it means for the church to be the church.

Contents

✝

Preface

✝

This book is for anyone who cares about the church. It began with a leadership retreat held in January of 1999; I had been asked to guide my fellow pastors and elders at Philadelphia's Tenth Presbyterian Church in a discussion about our future in ministry. What was God calling us to do as a church for the twenty-first century? How could we fulfill the calling Christ gave us to be "a city on a hill"?

Tenth is a thriving downtown church with an increasingly diverse congregation and a growing urban outreach. For nearly two hundred years, we have tried to reach our city and our world with the good news of God's transforming grace in Jesus Christ. The more I thought about the unique challenges we were likely to face over the next hundred years, the more convinced I became that we needed to keep pursuing the same priorities in ministry. As a church we have long been committed to the faithful exposition of God's Word, the reverent celebration of God in worship, the worldwide missionary work of Christ, and the practical application of divine mercy to the needs of our city. Did these priorities need to change? Quite the opposite. The changing face of American culture seemed to make these commitments more necessary than ever.

In 2001 I succeeded the late Dr. James Montgomery Boice as Tenth's senior minister. I began my ministry by preaching a series of sermons based on the seven commitments we make in our church mission statement. Those messages, which in many ways grew out of our earlier discussions about being a church for the twenty-first century, form the basis for this book. Obviously, they reflect some of the unique challenges and opportunities we experience in Center City Philadelphia. However, we believe our priorities are squarely based on Scripture, and thus that our mission statement has relevance for other churches in other settings.

This is not a book about ministry methods and management techniques (although the action guide gives help in some practical areas of church life). Instead, this book offers something more important: a theology of ministry. These days it is not uncommon to hear Christians say, "It's not about theology; it's about ministry." But of course ministry is always about theology. How we "do church" inevitably reflects our fundamental convictions about the Word of God, the gospel of Jesus Christ, and the ministry of the Holy Spirit. As we live for Christ in increasingly post-Christian times, it becomes more important than ever to know the biblical pattern for the church.

As always, with the publication of this book, I thank God for the love of my family, the prayers of our congregation, and the practical assistance offered by our administrative staff. The church session generously provided the study week I needed to revise the manuscript for final publication. I am also grateful to Jim Bell, Cheryl Dunlop, and the other editorial staff at Moody Publishers for pursuing this project.

Many friends were kind enough to review my manuscript and make suggestions for its improvement. Some are fellow ministers, including Steve DeWitt and Meredith Wheeler. Others are colleagues at Tenth Presbyterian Church, including David Apple, Cora Hogue, and Paul Jones. Still others are members of our church session, including Al Chapman, David Collins, David Skeel, and Joe Winston. Several friends went above and beyond the call of duty. Tim Keller, the founder of Manhattan's Redeemer Presbyterian Church, offered a rigorous critique. So did Mark Dever, whose talented staff at Capitol Hill Baptist Church in Washington devoted valuable time to reading and discussing my work. I am especially grateful to Jonathan Olsen and the other members of Tenth's pastoral staff for helping prepare the action guide at the end of the book.

Our prayer is that this book will help you glorify God in the church of Jesus Christ, which, like a great city on a high hill, cannot be hidden.

Philip Graham Ryken
Tenth Presbyterian Church
Philadelphia, Pennsylvania

I

The Church in the Twenty-first Century

✝

An Overview

> *"We have grown in numbers, wealth, and power as no other nation. But we have forgotten God."*
>
> —ᴼ ABRAHAM LINCOLN

We are living in post-Christian times. By this I do not mean that there aren't enough churches in America. There are. Our towns and cities are full of buildings designed for the worship of God, and in some cases still used for that purpose. Nor do I mean that there aren't very many Christians in America. We still have plenty of those, too. The vast majority of Americans believe in the existence of God, and many claim to be "born again." Nevertheless, we are living in post-Christian times, when Christianity no longer exercises a prevailing influence on the mind and heart of our culture.

There was a time when America *was* a Christian nation, at least in several important respects. There was a time when the leaders of this New World sought to establish a "city on a hill," a community for Christ and His kingdom. There was a time when our fundamental notions of freedom and justice were firmly embedded in the bedrock of biblical truth. There was a time when the Bible held a central place in the curriculum of the public schools and when our leading universities cultivated the Christian mind. There was a time when average Americans knew their Bibles well enough that biblical teaching had a strong influence on what people thought and how they behaved. In short, there was a time when Christianity shaped the social, political, moral, religious, and intellectual landscape of these United States.

We should be careful not to glamorize the past. From the very beginning, our nation was corrupted by sin, especially through the institution of slavery. And the church has always been weakened by nominal Christianity. So although it is true that America in some ways was a Christian nation, in other ways it was also a non-Christian nation.[1] Yet in spite of our past failings, we cannot help but lament the passing of a time when God still mattered in American life.

THE NEW BARBARISM

Now the barbarians are at the gates. Charles Colson has made the provocative statement that

> today in the West, and particularly in America, the new barbarians are all around us. They are not hairy Goths and Vandals, swilling fermented brew and ravishing maidens; they are not Huns and Visigoths storming our borders or scaling our city walls. No, this time the invaders have come from within. We have bred them in our families and trained them in our classrooms. They inhabit our legislatures, our courts, our film studios, and our churches. Most of them are attractive and pleasant; their ideas are persuasive and subtle. Yet these men and

women threaten our most cherished institutions and our very character as a people.[2]

There are many ways to prove that American culture is under attack from this new barbarism. One is to review the titles of the books that thoughtful people are writing: *Amusing Ourselves to Death, Slouching Towards Gomorrah, The Culture of Disbelief, No Place for Truth, The Twilight of American Culture, The End of Democracy.* Needless to say, the authors of these books are not optimistic about the future of American culture. Another way to see what is happening is to watch television, with its voyeuristic presentation of sexuality and suffering. Still another way to show that our nation is in trouble is to study the cold, hard statistics: the breakdown of marriage and family, the rise in crime and violence, the decline in community involvement. Then there is the callous disregard for life at the margins—in the womb and at the nursing home.

Meanwhile, we are moving faster and faster, always buying more products and constantly demanding better entertainment. And as we live in this Late Great Planet Hollywood, we are too distracted to notice what is happening to us spiritually. "Don't you understand, Richard?" asks a character in Douglas Coupland's *Girlfriend in a Coma.* "There is nothing at the center of what we do . . . no center. It doesn't exist. All of us—look at our lives: we have an acceptable level of affluence. We have entertainment. We have a relative freedom from fear. But there's nothing else."[3] The reason there is "nothing else" is that the new barbarism leaves no place for the soul.

The new barbarians do not look very threatening, at least from the outside. They do not wear animal skins or bang on the cultural gates with wooden clubs; instead, they talk on their cell phones and drink designer coffee. And, of course, they would not think of themselves as barbarians. But what is on their minds and in their hearts? Whether they admit it or not, their minds reject absolute truth, and in their hearts they love themselves more than anyone else, especially God. To use more precise terms, these post-Christian times are characterized by relativism and narcissism. And this is barbaric to the extent that it signals the death of a culture based on objective truth and civic virtue.

Relativism is radical skepticism, the rejection of absolute truth. It is the view that reality itself depends upon one's perspective. In the tongue-in-cheek words of British poet Steve Turner, "We believe that each man must find the truth that is right for him. Reality will adapt accordingly."[4] No one knows anything with objective certainty; it all depends on your point of view. This is part of what people mean by "postmodernism," and it represents a global shift in the way people think about truth and meaning. You have your story, and I have my story, but there is no divinely ordained story that ties them all together. The only absolute is that there are no absolutes. Your worldview is simply your opinion.

One of the troubling results of relativism is the erosion of traditional ethical and intellectual standards for science, law, medicine, journalism, and the use of technology. And when it comes to theology, relativism means that no religion can claim to be superior to any other faith. Each religion is true in its own way. Therefore, if Christianity is true at all, it is only relatively true. Exclusive claims like "the Bible is God's authoritative Word" or "Jesus Christ is the only Savior" must be rejected out of hand. In fact, the people who make such claims are probably dangerous.

Narcissism is radical individualism, or infatuation with the self. In ancient Greek mythology, Narcissus was the beautiful youth who fell in love with his reflection. As he sat beside the pool, gazing longingly at his own image, he wasted away and died, and was transformed into a flower. There has always been a narcissistic tendency in American culture, but we are now entering an era of radical selfishness and unbridled individualism. What is new is that being self-centered is now considered a virtue. According to Robert Schuller, "Self-love is, or should be, the basic will in human life."[5]

When people think this way (as many people do), they feel justified in doing whatever seems to be in their self-interest, without showing much compassion or giving much consideration to their neighbors, co-workers, employees, spouses, or children. We live in a culture of takers, not givers. In his landmark study *The Culture of Narcissism*, sociologist Christopher Lasch discovered that ordinary Americans now display many of the same character traits that are usually associated with pathological personality disorders. Narcissism has become normal.[6] One sign of our self-absorption is that it is becoming increasingly difficult for our nation to do anything that requires widespread cooperation or personal sacrifice, such as combat poverty, improve education, reform our health system, or provide for the common defense.

Taken together, the relativistic mind and the narcissistic heart explain a good deal about what is wrong with America today. People who do not know what is true (or who wonder if anything is true at all) are unable to do what is right and just and good. Intellectual skepticism quickly leads to moral relativism. And because people who live for themselves are unable to establish loving communities, many Americans end up feeling alienated and abandoned. In the rising generation there is a deep pessimism about the possibility of love and romance, to say nothing of marriage and family.

As we reflect on America's cultural situation in the twenty-first century, we appear to be living in the times that the apostle Paul described for Timothy when he said: "Mark this: There will be terrible times in the last days. People will be lovers of themselves . . . lovers of pleasure rather than lovers of God. . . . For the time will come when men will not put up with sound doctrine" (2 Tim. 3:1, 2a, 4b; 4:3a). What Paul said serves as an apt description of our own narcissistic and relativistic times, when people serve themselves and are skeptical of the possibility of truth.

Historians now generally regard the twentieth century as the American Century. It is too early to tell what they will call the next hundred years, but in America it may well be the first post-Christian century. Of course, it is always possible that a new wave of reformation and revival will sweep across our land. Then again, our country may come to a sudden and catastrophic end, precipitated by an energy crisis, a financial meltdown, or an enemy attack. But what seems most likely is that what is perhaps the most powerful nation in the history of the world will undergo a long, slow, demoralizing decline before finally collapsing under the weight of its own decadence.

NOW HOW SHALL WE LIVE?

It is understandable for Christians to be dismayed by what is happening in America and to be pessimistic about its prospects for the future. However, as Christians it is not our responsibility to save our culture, if indeed it ought to be saved. So this is not a book about trying to recover the past. But we do need to discern what is happening in America so that we know what it means to live for Christ in our times. As our civilization continues to decline, the church will have unprecedented opportunities to show the world what a difference it makes to be a Christian. The question is, How should a Christian live in post-Christian times? What does it mean to be a city on a hill today?

The temptation is to think that we need to find a new way

of "doing church." This is exactly what happened in the last decades of the twentieth century. Many evangelicals were scrambling around trying to find something that would work. They realized that America was in trouble and that the traditional denominations were in decline, so they tried to make Christianity more relevant. They got involved in politics, lobbying against abortion and trying to get prayer back into the public schools. They entered business by marketing Christianity to the masses, turning Christ into a commodity. They even tried their hand at entertainment, seeking to make their services appeal to a secular audience.

Some church leaders think a pragmatic approach is necessary. Peter Wagner, the guru of the church growth movement, writes,

> The greatest change in the way of doing church since the Protestant reformation is taking place before our very eyes. . . . The radical change in the sixteenth century was largely theological. The current reformation is not so much a reformation of faith (the essential theological principles of the Reformation are intact), but a reformation of practice. A major difference was that the sixteenth century reformation came in reaction to a corrupt and apostate church. This current reformation is not so much against corruption and apostasy as it is against irrelevance.[7]

If irrelevance is the enemy, then churches constantly have to figure out how to stay relevant. Wagner offers a number of suggestions for doing this, but perhaps the most significant is reducing theology to the shortest possible list of essential doctrines. Theological instruction is said to be irrelevant, especially if it is thorough and precise. This is in sharp contrast to the original Reformation, which was all about theology. The Protestant mottoes were *sola gratia, sola fide, solus Christus,* and *soli Deo gloria:* Salvation is by grace alone, through faith alone, in

Christ alone, so that God alone gets all the glory. This is what the reformers taught because they believed in *sola Scriptura*—Scripture alone—which is where all these great doctrines are found. What, then, is the motto of the so-called new reformation? At times it seems as if some churches are opting for *fiat quidvis efficiens:* "Do whatever works."

When churches make relevance their primary goal, they are vulnerable to the twin perils of postmodernism: relativism and narcissism. They succumb to relativism because they are willing to sacrifice biblical principles for popular success. And they are guilty of narcissism because they crave the acceptance of secular society, as if "the interests and ambitions of the unconverted can somehow be harnessed to win their approval for Christ."[8]

I do not think for a moment that the church should aspire to become *ir*relevant. There is always a need for Christians to speak the gospel into their own context. Rather, my concern is with the ever-present danger of *over*-contextualizing. Consider what happens to a church that is always trying to appeal to an increasingly post-Christian culture. Almost inevitably, the church itself becomes post-Christian. This is what happened to the liberal church during the twentieth century, and it is what is happening to the evangelical church right now. As James Montgomery Boice has argued, evangelicals are accepting the world's wisdom, embracing the world's theology, adopting the world's agenda, and employing the world's methods.[9] In theology a revision of evangelical doctrine is now underway that seeks to bring Christianity more in line with postmodern thought.[10] The obvious difficulty is that in a post-Christian culture, a church that tries too hard to be "relevant" may in the process lose its very identity as the church. Rather than confronting the world, the church gets co-opted by it. It no longer stands a city on a hill, but sinks to the level of the surrounding culture.

So what should we do? The leaders of the so-called new reformation begin with the future and then look to the present. This is in contrast with traditional church leaders, who begin with the present and then look to the past. So where should we look? If we only look to the future, we run the risk of abandoning our spiritual heritage. However, if we look to the past, then we may live in the past, and thereby fail to serve God effectively in our own times. What we should do instead is live in the present, learn from the past, and anticipate the future, while always looking to the Bible.

THE FIRST-CENTURY CHURCH

When we look to the Bible we see God's plan for the church at all times and in all places. So to understand how to live for Christ in the twenty-first century, we need to go back to the first century. This is not traditionalism; it is not irrelevance; it is not living in the past. It is timeless Christianity, which is founded on Jesus Christ, who is the same yesterday and today and forever (Heb. 13:8).

The first church was founded on the gospel. After Jesus of Nazareth was crucified, raised from the dead, and ascended back to heaven, His followers remained in Jerusalem. God poured out His Holy Spirit and they began to preach. Their message was salvation in Jesus Christ. They spoke of His atoning death, how Christ died on the cross for sinners. They emphasized the reality of Christ's resurrection and exaltation, coming to this climax: "God has made this Jesus, whom you crucified, both Lord and Christ" (Acts 2:36).

People responded the way sinners ought to respond when they learn about the grace that God offers in Jesus Christ. Their hearts melted and they asked what they should do. The apostle Peter told them to turn away from their sins and put their faith in Christ. He said, "Repent and be baptized, every one of you, in the name of Jesus Christ for the forgiveness of your sins" (Acts 2:38). He pleaded with them, "Save yourselves from this corrupt generation" (Acts 2:40).

That last statement is significant because it shows that the first Christians lived in the same times that we live in. Not exactly the same, of course, because they were pre-Christian rather than post-Christian. But like us, they were living in a corrupt culture, and thus they can show us what it means to live for Christ in declining times. Here is what they did:

> They devoted themselves to the apostles' teaching and to the fellowship, to the breaking of bread and to prayer. Everyone was filled with awe, and many wonders and miraculous signs were done by the apostles. All the believers were together and had everything in common. Selling their possessions and goods, they gave to anyone as he had need. Every day they continued to meet together in the temple courts. They broke bread in their homes and ate together with glad and sincere hearts, praising God and enjoying the favor of all the people. And the Lord added to their number daily those who were being saved. (Acts 2:42–47)

The first Christians were saved by turning to Jesus in faith and repentance. Once they were saved, they formed a teaching, worshiping, and caring community that, by the grace of God, also became a growing community.

A Teaching Church

It is significant that teaching is mentioned first, because everything else depends on the plain teaching of God's Word. It is the Word that establishes the church by bringing people to a saving knowledge of Jesus Christ. It is the Word that teaches us how to worship, defines the sacraments, and sets the agenda for prayer. It is the Word that instructs us to love one another and teaches us how to care. It all flows from God's Word, which means that a teaching church will enjoy every blessing of God's Spirit.

The first Christians *devoted* themselves to the teaching of the apostles: "Every day they continued to meet together in the temple courts" (Acts 2:46a). One of their primary reasons for meeting was to learn the apostolic doctrine, which is what is meant by the word "teaching." The first-century church was hungry for biblical and theological instruction.

In the twenty-first century we cannot go to the temple and hear the apostles in person. There is a way to devote ourselves to their teaching, however, and that is by studying the Bible. As Peter's preaching demonstrates, the apostles based their gospel presentation on the Hebrew Scriptures. Thus one way to follow their example is by studying, teaching, and applying the Old Testament. What the apostles preached was the good news about Jesus Christ, so of course it is also necessary to know the New Testament Gospels. Then there is the apostolic doctrine itself, which is contained in Acts, the Epistles, and Revelation. The teaching of the apostles thus spans the Scriptures, which means that anyone devoted to their teaching studies the whole Bible.

The only church that will survive in post-Christian times is a church with a passion for God's Word. This means reading the Bible, both privately and in services of public worship. It means preaching the Bible by way of systematic exposition. It means studying the Bible, chapter by chapter and verse by verse. It means teaching the Bible, so that every group and every ministry in the church is guided and directed by the voice of God's Spirit speaking in Scripture. It is not enough to have a high doctrine of Scripture; the church must also make regular use of Scripture. A church for post-Christian times is a teaching church—a church that longs to know God's mind as revealed in God's Word.

A Worshiping Church

A church for post-Christian times is also a worshiping church. This is what the first Christians meant by "the fellowship": "They devoted themselves . . . to the fellowship, to the breaking of bread and to prayer" (Acts 2:42). The Greek word for fellowship is *koinonia,* which means "sharing" or "participation." Here it seems to refer specifically to their participation in public worship, including prayer and the sacraments.

The early church constantly gathered for worship. Every day the first Christians went at set times to the temple courts. There, in addition to hearing the apostles preach, they sang psalms and said their prayers in Jesus' name. They also worshiped in smaller groups from house to house: "They broke bread in their homes and ate together with glad and sincere hearts, praising God" (Acts 2:46–47a). Privately as well as publicly, they enjoyed fellowship in its truest and richest sense, joining their minds and their hearts to give glory to God.

The application is obvious. A Christian church for post-Christian times must exalt God in its worship. As much as anything else, what defines a church is its public assembly in the presence of God. A local church is a *congregation*—a group of believers who gather around God's throne to offer Him their praise and thanksgiving. The reason worship is at the center of church life is that in worship, God is placed at the center of our attention. This is true not only of corporate worship, but also of private and family worship.

"The fellowship," as the apostles called it, included prayer as well as "the breaking of bread." The first Christians were always getting together to pray, especially in times of uncertainty or persecution (e.g., Acts 1:14; 4:24; 12:12). Prayer was part of their daily routine, not only privately, but also in public worship at the temple. They prayed because they understood that they could accomplish nothing without the work of God's Spirit.

The "breaking of bread" is of course *the* breaking of bread: the Lord's Supper. This sacrament is a great mystery containing many deep truths of the gospel. It is much more than a remembrance of Christ's atoning death; by the presence of His Holy Spirit it is also a participation in His resurrection life. But what is emphasized in Acts 2 is that the Lord's Supper is a communal meal. By eating the bread and drinking the cup, Christians are separated from the world and set apart as the community of God's people. In this connection it is worth noticing that verse 47 refers to the "number" of believers. This hints at something that can be demonstrated elsewhere in the New Testament, namely, that the first-century church practiced formal membership and discipline. This was essential if Christians were to maintain their distinct identity as the people of God.

All of these things remain necessary for the church in the twenty-first century. If we belong to Christ, then we must belong to His church. We must devote ourselves to public and private worship. We must celebrate the sacraments, reaffirming not only our commitment to Christ, but also our participation in His body, the church. And we must remain committed to prayer, asking God to do in us, for us, and through us what we cannot do for ourselves.

A Caring Church

Earlier I mentioned *koinonia*, which means sharing or fellowship. Besides corporate worship, there is another kind of sharing that Christians enjoy: the sharing of burdens. Like the first-century church, a church for post-Christian times is a sharing, caring church.

There are really only three attitudes that a person can take toward material possessions. The thief says, "What's yours is mine; I'll take it." The selfish person says, "What's mine is mine; I'll keep it." But the caring person says, "What's mine is really God's, and so I'll share it."[11] And that is exactly what Christians did in the first century. They made a radical commitment to Christian community, which included a willingness to give time and money to meet one another's needs: "All the believers were together and had everything in common. Selling their possessions and goods, they gave to anyone as he had need" (Acts 2:44–45). We read further in chapter 4, "All the believers were one in heart and mind. No one claimed that any of his possessions was his own, but they shared everything they had. . . . There were no needy persons among them. For from time to time those who owned lands or houses sold them, brought the money from the sales and put it at the apostles' feet, and it was distributed to anyone as he had need" (Acts 4:32, 34–35).

This is a remarkable testimony to God's grace in the church. The first Christians had one heart and one mind. They had a deep sense of spiritual unity that was based on their common faith in Jesus Christ. This made them willing to sell their property and share their possessions to meet the needs of the poor.

This is all the more remarkable when we remember how diverse Jerusalem was in those days. Among the first people to hear and receive the gospel were "Jews from every nation under heaven" (Acts 2:5). There were both women and men, for in his sermon Peter said the gathering fulfilled the prophecy, "Your sons and daughters will prophesy" (Acts 2:17). The gospel was for children as well as adults, for Peter also said, "The promise is for you and your children and for all who are far off" (Acts 2:39). When Peter said "far off," this included the Gentiles. So the first-century church was a multi-ethnic, multi-national, multi-generational community that was united by its faith in Jesus Christ, and thus committed to care for anyone in need.

A Growing Church

Notice the result: Outsiders were impressed by this caring community and wanted to join. The Scripture says that the first Christians enjoyed "the favor of all the people. And the Lord added to their number daily those who were being saved" (Acts 2:47). By the grace of God, a teaching, worshiping, and caring church also becomes a growing church.

The first-century church was unique in this respect, for it grew more rapidly than perhaps any other church in history. In order to confirm the truth of His Word, God empowered the apostles to perform miracles (Acts 2:43) and greatly blessed their preaching. Peter's first sermon led to the conversion of more than three thousand people! And that was only the beginning, for "the Lord added to their number daily those who were being saved" (Acts 2:47b). Needless to say, these are not events that every local church can reproduce. Yet the principle here is valid at all times and in all places: A church that follows the biblical pattern in preaching, worship, and fellowship will be fruitful in outreach and evangelism.

The Bible says relatively little about the evangelistic efforts of average Christians during the age of the apostles. It is not hard to guess what they did, however. For them evangelism was not so much a special event or a practiced method as it was an integral part of their overall life as a church. They invited their friends and family members to hear the apostles preach. They shared with neighbors in need. As they had opportunity, they testified to their own personal faith in Jesus Christ. They engaged their community mind to mind, heart to heart, and life to life. Their God-centered way of living inevitably had a way of pointing people to Christ. People outside the church looked up on the hill and saw God's city. And as they experienced the attractive power of authentic Christian community, many of them accepted Jesus as their Savior and Lord.

The evangelical church has begun to decline, and it is hard to imagine how it can grow in the twenty-first century. But there is a biblical method for church growth. It is to become a teaching, worshiping, caring church. Such a church has God's approval, and with His blessing, it will grow.

WHAT THE WORLD NEEDS

The charter members of the first church in Jerusalem were a remarkable group of men and women. By the power of God's Spirit they turned the world upside down, starting the most remarkable institution in human history. Yet anyone who has ever been to a good church cannot help but notice that what they did was thoroughly ordinary. There was Bible reading and preaching. There was corporate worship, including prayer and the sacraments. There was fellowship and evangelism. They simply did the things that Christians since them have always done— which is exactly the point! Wherever Christians have joined together to establish teaching, worshiping, and caring communities, they have been able to meet the unique challenges they faced from the surrounding culture.

We see this throughout church history. During the Roman Empire when Caesar was throwing Christians to the lions, during the Middle Ages when spiritual darkness descended on Europe, during the twentieth century when Communism tried to stamp out any mention of God—at all times and in all places —Christians have "devoted themselves to the apostles' teaching and to the fellowship, to the breaking of bread and to prayer"

(Acts 2:42). Today a Christian can go anywhere in the world and meet brothers and sisters who are doing the same thing. Whether they meet in public or in secret, whether they gather in great cathedrals or small house churches, they are teaching, worshiping, caring . . . and growing. What God has given us in the church will last as long as life on this earth. For Jesus said, "I will build my church, and the gates of Hades will not overcome it" (Matt. 16:18).

Here in America, as we enter our first post-Christian century, some churches will continue to do the simple things that churches have always done. And as they do so, they will discover that what God has given in the church is exactly what a post-Christian culture needs.

The prevailing mind-set is relativism, the denial of universal truth. The way to respond is by remaining devoted to the apostolic teaching of Scripture. People are looking for some other message, delivered by some other means. However, what God has appointed for the salvation of sinners and for their subsequent growth in grace is the preaching of the gospel, together with the teaching of biblical doctrine. This is God's permanent plan for the church. It also happens to be the perfect antihistamine for a culture that is allergic to truth.

The heart of post-Christian culture is narcissistic, but the Bible has a remedy for self-infatuation: God-glorifying, Christ-centered, Spirit-filled worship. In worship we turn away from ourselves to adore the Father, the Son, and the Holy Spirit. Once our hearts have turned to God in prayer and praise, we are then able to reach out to others in love and concern. This kind of Christian caring is the answer to many, if not most, contemporary problems. It is the answer to the breakup of the family, for in a caring church people learn how to keep commitments that put others first. It is the answer to racism, for a caring church is united by Christ across the things that divide. It is the answer to poverty, for in a caring church all needs are met, including the deepest needs of the soul. Whether people realize it or not, what our crumbling culture needs most is authentic Christian community.

To summarize, what God wants the church to be and to do turns out to be exactly what the world needs. Admittedly, the world may not want to hear it, since in post-Christian times the church becomes a kind of countercultural community. To a relativistic culture, skeptical of meaning, the church preaches the truth of God's eternal Word. To a narcissistic culture, alienated by sin, the church issues an invitation to worship and fellowship. And this is precisely what a post-Christian culture needs: a church that stands out as truly Christian.

A CHURCH FOR CHRIST

Why does it work out this way? Why is it that what the church is called to do turns out to be what the world needs most? The answer is that everything the church does centers on Jesus Christ, and this is what the world always needs: to know Jesus Christ as Savior and Lord. Each of the church's essential, Bible-based activities finds its meaning in His person and work.

A church for post-Christian times is a teaching church, a church devoted to the apostolic message. And what did the apostles preach? They preached Jesus Christ—crucified, buried, and risen. They preached Jesus Christ as Savior from sin, Lord of all creation, and the answer to every need. The apostle Paul said, "Jews demand miraculous signs and Greeks look for wisdom, but we preach Christ crucified: a stumbling block to Jews and foolishness to Gentiles, but to those whom God has called, both Jews and Greeks, Christ the power of God and the wisdom of God" (1 Cor. 1:22–24).

A church for post-Christian times is a worshiping church.

But on what basis can we approach God—in all His holiness—to give Him our praise? Only on the basis of the perfect righteousness and atoning death of Jesus Christ. And when we come to worship God, we come offering praise to Christ as our Savior and Lord. We offer prayer and perform baptism in His name. And in the Lord's Supper we remember His sufferings and death, as we wait for His triumphant return. True Christian worship is always given to the glory of God in the name of Jesus Christ.

A church for post-Christian times is a caring church, and what enables us to care and to share is the love of Jesus Christ. Whenever we serve, help, pray for, encourage, and even rebuke one another, we are demonstrating His love. To summarize, when the church does what it is supposed to do, everything it does exalts the name of Jesus Christ. The result is a growing church, a church that God will use to bring people to know Him in a saving way.

These basic biblical priorities can be summarized in a single purpose statement: For the honor of Jesus Christ, a twenty-first century church needs to develop and maintain a strong teaching pulpit, an effective network of fellowship groups aimed at meeting individual needs, a program of Christian education to promote the steady growth of God's family to spiritual maturity, and, in cooperation with other Christians, an evangelistic outreach to the local community and to the world beyond.

This purpose statement, which is adapted from the one used by Philadelphia's Tenth Presbyterian Church, can be further specified in seven objectives:

- to uphold a tradition of strong expository preaching by gifted men of God
- to worship God in a worthy manner through thoughtful words, devoted prayers, and excellent music

- to integrate every member of the congregation into Bible studies and other groups where individual needs can be met and each can minister to others
- to supply loving pastoral care for each member of the church family
- to provide an effective Christian education program to inform, train, and disciple all members of the congregation
- to advance the missionary work of the church in the local community and throughout the world
- to serve the church and its community through ministries of mercy

These seven objectives form the basis for the rest of this book. I believe that they are biblical mandates for the Christian church at every time, in every place. If so, then they can show us what it means to live for Christ in these post-Christian times, standing like a city on a hill.

2

Making
God's Word Plain

✝

Expository Preaching

> *"Preaching must be plain. . . . It is a by-word among us:*
> *'It was a very plain sermon.' And I say, the plainer, the better."*
>
> —⌐ WILLIAM PERKINS

Preaching has fallen out of favor. "Stop preaching at me," people say in these post-Christian times. "Spare me the sermon." If we consult the dictionary, we find that the first definition of preach is "to deliver a sermon," but the second is "to exhort in a . . . tiresome manner." And when average Americans think of preaching, that is exactly what they have in mind: Christian communication that is almost certainly boring and probably annoying as well.

Preaching is also falling out of favor among Christians, which is yet another sign that our post-Christian culture is producing a post-Christian church. The listener, not God, is sovereign. There is an overall "dumbing down" of doctrine. Sermons are getting shorter; if they go longer than twenty minutes, people start to get restless. Church-goers demand to be entertained, so in some cases the sermon is gradually replaced by music, testimonies, drama, or even video. Where there is a strong commitment to preaching, it often tends to be more experiential than biblical and more humanistic than evangelistic. One popular trend is for preachers to tell "a simple story designed to teach a moral lesson, as opposed to a traditional dissection of a biblical text. Often it is a very personal tale of the preacher's trials and triumphs, with lots of emotional content and little thorny theology."[1] Ministers who resort to this form of communication have lost their confidence in the power of God's Word. As a result, their congregations rarely hear the voice of God's Spirit speaking in Scripture. The post-Christian church no longer believes in the power of biblical preaching, plain and simple.

A decline in preaching is always disastrous, because the sermon is a divinely ordained means for bringing sinners to Christ. Consider this biblical line of reasoning: "'Everyone who calls on the name of the Lord will be saved.' How, then, can they call on the one they have not believed in? And how can they believe in the one of whom they have not heard? And how can they hear without someone preaching to them?" (Rom. 10:13–14). By the sheer force of logic, we are forced to admit that without hearing the Word preached, sinners cannot be saved. In these post-Christian times ministers are sometimes told to stop preaching to the unchurched. Yet gospel preaching is a necessary part of God's plan for their salvation.

Preaching is equally necessary for the Christian life. The gospel is not a form of self-help; it is a transforming message. Thus it is through the explanation and proclamation of God's Word—with exhortation—that believers grow in grace. Therefore, what the church needs in these post-Christian times is preaching—biblical, expositional, practical preaching that proclaims Christ from all the Scriptures.

No Tolerance for Truth

In the preceding chapter, we identified two significant features of spiritual life in the twenty-first century: relativism and narcissism. Relativism is the denial of absolute meaning. The relativist says, "The truth is whatever you want it to be." Narcissism is the worship of the self. The narcissist asks, "What's in it for me?"

If we are living in an age of relativism and narcissism, then what are the implications for preaching? Obviously, Bible teaching will be out of favor. Sinners generally do not like to have their selfishness exposed; but that is one of the primary purposes of preaching the Bible. In a post-Christian culture, the last thing people want to hear is the truth about their self-centeredness. What preaching there is, therefore, tends to be therapeutic rather than prophetic. It aims to make people feel better about who they are rather than to challenge them to become, by God's grace, what they are not. But most people can be counted on not to want anyone to preach to them at all. The apostle Paul anticipated this centuries ago. To Timothy he wrote, "The time will come when men will not put up with sound doctrine. Instead, to suit their own desires, they will gather around them a great number of teachers to say what their itching ears want to hear" (2 Tim. 4:3).

When Paul said "the time will come," what time did he have in mind? Probably the whole time between the first and second comings of Christ, between His resurrection and His return, which would include our own post-Christian times. The twenty-first century is one of the times when "men will not put up with sound doctrine." They simply will not tolerate it. They will not have the patience to listen to theological instruction. And when they do hear what the Bible says, they will deny that it is truth from God. Instead, they will believe whatever they want to believe, listening only to teachers who tell them whatever they want to hear, so that they can do whatever they want to do. As the Scripture says, "They will turn their ears away from the truth and turn aside to myths" (2 Tim. 4:4).

The word "myth" sounds rather primitive. People today do not still believe in *myths*, do they? Of course they do. A myth is any popular belief that guides human thought and conduct but is not based on God's truth. There is the myth of individualism, the idea that I can make it on my own. There is the myth of victimization, that my personal problems are due primarily or exclusively to the sins of others. There is the myth of materialism, the assumption that there is always something I can buy that will make me happy. Then there is the grand myth of evolutionism, the belief that, in the words of one Harvard scientist, "Man is the result of a purposeless and natural process that did not have him in mind."[2] These are some of the myths of our times—popular yet unbiblical beliefs that shape the way Americans think and act.

THE NEW EVANGELICALISM

When the apostle Paul spoke about myths, however, he was not referring primarily to ideas in the general culture, but to what people were thinking in the church. His concern was with those who had a form of godliness, yet denied its power (2 Tim. 3:5). In other words, he was worried about people who called themselves Christians but did not know Christ, who were unorthodox in their theology and unbiblical in their practice. All of which leads us to ask this question: What dangerous doctrines confront the contemporary church? Each generation faces its own theological challenges, so it is necessary to identify the ideas that threaten to harm the church in the twenty-first century.

The winds of doctrinal change are already sweeping through the evangelical church. Some colleges and seminaries are heading in the direction of what has been termed "post-conservative" evangelicalism. The new evangelicals move beyond the boundaries of the historic confessions, in some cases by introducing postmodern perspectives to Christianity. The following doctrines are coming under attack:

The Doctrine of Scripture

This was an area of dispute throughout the twentieth century, culminating with "the Battle for the Bible." In many churches the battle was won on behalf of infallibility and inerrancy—the Bible cannot and does not err. Yet the war may still be lost. Today there is widespread ignorance about what the Bible actually teaches. Even those who believe that Scripture is true deny that it is sufficient for evangelism, guidance, spiritual growth, or social change.[3] They say that in addition to Scripture, other methods and techniques are needed. Then there are the many evangelical Bible scholars whose hermeneutical assumptions and exegetical methods are virtually indistinguishable from those employed by liberal scholars. The evangelical doctrine of biblical inerrancy is becoming notional rather than foundational.

The Doctrine of God

There is a growing movement among some evangelicals to advocate the "openness of God," or "open theism." (It is, of course, questionable whether it is still legitimate for them to lay claim to the title "evangelical.") This is an attempt to solve the mystery of divine sovereignty and human responsibility by denying that God has full knowledge of the future. The new evangelical deity is a risk-taker whose will is sometimes thwarted and whose plans often change in response to the actions of human beings. This doctrine of God is purported to be more faithful to the Scriptures. However, it is a radical departure from biblically orthodox teaching about divine foreknowledge. The true God is all-knowing. He says, "I am God, and there is no other; I am God, and there is none like me. I make known the end from the beginning, from ancient times, what is still to come" (Isa. 46:9–10).

The Doctrine of Christ

Here the trend is toward religious relativism. Many people believe that all religions are equally true, that they all provide equally valid perspectives on ultimate reality. In the church this takes the form of denying that Jesus is the only way to God. To-day some scholars who claim to be evangelicals nevertheless claim that explicit personal faith in Jesus Christ is unnecessary for salvation. Under the influence of other world religions, they conclude that God must also offer forgiveness through non-Christian religions. Jesus Christ is one possible expression of salvation, but not its exclusive means. Or they say that although Jesus is the only Savior, different people come to Him in different ways, sometimes without explicitly knowing who He is. This is yet another example of the way a post-Christian culture produces a post-Christian church. The truth is that God really does require faith in Jesus Christ for salvation. It is only by be-lieving in Him that anyone will not perish, but receive everlast-ing life (John 3:16). "Salvation is found in no one else, for there is no other name under heaven given to men by which we must be saved" (Acts 4:12).

The Doctrine of Sin

People are prone to believe in their own basic goodness. In America this cause is advanced by the aggressive proclamation of the good news of self-esteem. People need to feel better about themselves, not worse. Or at least that's what some pastors think, so they tread but lightly on the toes of fallen sinners. They preach grace without ever preaching the law, self-acceptance without repentance. What is missing is an evangelically orthodox doctrine of humanity as created in God's image, fallen into depravity, and spiritually dead apart from the regenerating work of God's Spirit.

The Doctrine of Salvation

Evangelicals are forgetting and in some cases denying vital Reformation teaching on the doctrine of justification. Partly out of an eagerness to find common cause with Catholicism, and also as the result of a new perspective on Paul and the Law, post-conservative evangelicals dismiss the necessity or even the possibility of receiving Christ's righteousness by faith alone. The biblical view is that God imputes or credits His righteousness to the believer, so that when we stand before Him we are covered with the perfect righteousness of Jesus Christ (see Rom. 3:21–24). We are not justified by anything we do for ourselves, but only what Christ has done for us (see Eph. 2:8–9). By contrast, the Roman Catholic view includes good works as part of the basis for our justification. And the new perspective on Paul and the Law downplays the centrality of justification for the New Testament gospel. Under these influences, some evangelicals are losing their grip on the Reformation principle of *sola fide*, the gospel of justification by faith alone.

These new theological trends are not peripheral matters, but strike at the very heart of Christian theology. They concern such fundamental doctrines as the sufficiency of Scripture, the sovereignty of God, the validity of Christ, the depravity of sin, and the necessity of divine righteousness. Unless these post-conservative doctrines are denied, they will destroy evangelical theology. Whereas the twentieth century witnessed the decline of liberalism, the twenty-first century may well see the end of evangelicalism as a coherent Christian movement.

How should the church respond to these challenges? In a time of widespread biblical ignorance and increasing doctrinal confusion, how can Christians maintain their theological integrity? The answer is very simple: "Preach the Word" (2 Tim. 4:2a).

THE WORD THAT IS PREACHED

What ministers are to preach is *the Word*—that is, the Word of God. A faithful minister does not preach the latest news. He does not preach his private opinion, his personal experience, or his political agenda. He does not even preach his own theological tradition, although of course he does preach within it, insofar as his system of doctrine is derived from Scripture. What he preaches is God's eternal, infallible Word, as written in the Scriptures of the Old and New Testaments.

What kind of Word is this? Paul reminded Timothy of several of its significant features. First, *the Word comes from God.* The Bible has a divine origin. People sometimes say that the Bible is inspired, and what they mean when they say "inspired" is true. Yet the Bible actually teaches that God's Word is "ex-spired." According to the original Greek, when the Bible says that "all Scripture is God-breathed" (2 Tim. 3:16a), it does not mean that God has simply breathed into Scripture, but that He has breathed it out. The Bible is the creative product of the Holy Spirit, and thus it bears God's own perfection and authority. Paul says "all Scripture" in order to show that each and every verse in the whole Bible is "ex-spired" in this way. This doctrine is sometimes called "plenary verbal inspiration." What it means is that all the words of Scripture are the very words of God, which is why we believe they are infallible and inerrant in the original manuscripts.

This is not to deny that the Bible was written by real human beings, who had their own experiences and abilities. Yet even these things were under God's sovereign control. The Bible is not merely a human book about God; it is God's book to humanity. Therefore, the Word the minister reads and preaches is God's own Word. It is fully trustworthy and absolutely true in every respect.

Second, *the Word brings salvation through faith in Christ.* This had been Timothy's own experience, as Paul reminded him: "But as for you, continue in what you have learned and have become convinced of, because you know those from whom you learned it, and how from infancy you have known the holy Scriptures, which are able to make you wise for salvation through faith in Christ Jesus" (2 Tim. 3:14–15). Timothy had been raised on the Bible. His mother and grandmother taught him the Scriptures of the Old Testament, and in time this brought him to a saving knowledge of Jesus Christ. God always sends His Word with this saving purpose. By the power of the Holy Spirit, the Word persuades sinners to turn away from their sins and convinces them to receive Christ as Savior and Lord.

The reason the Bible has this saving influence is that it is all about Jesus Christ. After He was raised from the dead, Jesus walked to Emmaus with two of His disciples, who were having trouble understanding the meaning of the crucifixion and who didn't yet believe the eyewitness accounts of the resurrection. Jesus wanted to help them, so "beginning with Moses and all the Prophets, he explained to them what was said in all the Scriptures concerning himself" (Luke 24:27). Not only is all Scripture God-breathed, but all Scripture is also Christ-centered. The salvation that was expected in the Old Testament is exhibited in the Gospels and then explained in the rest of the New Testament. From Genesis to Revelation, God's Word is all about Jesus, and thus it has the power to bring salvation through faith in Him.

The Bible does more than bring people to faith in Christ, however; it also helps them to grow in grace. So a third great truth is that *the Word prepares the Christian to do God's work.* Actually, this is the main thing that Paul wanted Timothy to know: "All Scripture is God-breathed and is useful for teaching, rebuking, correcting and training in righteousness, so that the man of God may be thoroughly equipped for every good work" (2 Tim. 3:16–17). This verse contains what may be the greatest understatement in the Bible: "Scripture is useful." Useful? You bet it's useful! Having been breathed out by God, it is of inestimable practical benefit for knowing and serving Him.

Paul uses four words to describe its usefulness—two that pertain to doctrine and two that pertain to life. God's Word is useful for *teaching*—in other words, for communicating theological truth. It is also useful for *rebuking*, which means to refute doctrinal error. Taken together, these terms show that the Bible distinguishes between truth and error in theology. Scripture is equally useful for *correcting*, which has to do with personal conduct. The Bible warns us away from sin, reproving our tendency to serve ourselves. More positively, it is profitable for *training in righteousness.* God's Word disciples us by teaching us the difference between the right way and the wrong way to live. To summarize, the Bible is useful for both doctrine and life, for creed as well as conduct. It is so useful that it provides total preparation for doing God's will. A Christian who knows the Bible is fully trained to serve God at home, at work, in the church, and everywhere else in a post-Christian culture.

PREACHING THE WORD

What the minister is to do with the Word—the Word from God that brings salvation and prepares the Christian to do God's work—is to preach it. And in his instructions to Timothy, the apostle Paul indicates what that preaching ought to include.

In the first place, preaching must be *evangelical*, which simply means that it takes as its central theme the gospel of Jesus Christ. The Greek word for preach *(kerygma)* is the word for proclamation. So when Paul told Timothy to preach, he was telling him to proclaim the good news of the gospel. A minister is a herald who makes the royal announcement of salvation through the death and resurrection of Jesus Christ.

Good preaching is always evangelistic, which perhaps is why Paul went on to remind Timothy to "do the work of an evangelist" (2 Tim. 4:5). Even though he was the pastor of an established church, Timothy still needed to reach the lost. Proclaiming the gospel was a necessary part of his ongoing work as a minister. A preacher is an evangelist who, in one way or another, is always saying to people, both in public and in private, "Believe in the Lord Jesus, and you will be saved" (Acts 16:31).

This kind of proclamation requires boldness, a virtue that is sadly lacking in the contemporary church. One of the reasons evangelicalism is in decline is that Christians have lost their nerve. In these post-Christian times, we are all too content to live in our own private enclaves, reinforcing our own opinions by attending our own schools, forming our own clubs, and reading our own magazines. However, it is not the herald's job to stay at home. His task is to go out and confront people with his message, which in this case is the most important message ever proclaimed: the free gift of eternal life through faith in Jesus Christ.

In addition to being evangelical, preaching must also be *doctrinal.* Preserving sound doctrine is a major emphasis in the pastoral epistles. According to Paul, anyone who wants to be a good minister must watch his doctrine closely (1 Tim. 4:16) and "correctly handle the word of truth" (2 Tim. 2:15). He must maintain "the truths of the faith" (1 Tim. 4:6), also described as "the sound instruction of our Lord Jesus Christ" (1 Tim. 6:3) and "the pattern of sound teaching" (2 Tim. 1:13).

Paul understood that the future of the church depends on the defense of its doctrine. When he charged Timothy to preach the Word, therefore, what he had in mind was the preaching of biblical doctrine. This is clear from the end of 2 Timothy 4:2, where Timothy is told to preach with "careful instruction," which again means "doctrine." The reason he needed to preach this way is given in the following verse: "For the time will come when men will not put up with sound doctrine" (2 Tim. 4:3). If the problem is unsound doctrine, then obviously the solution is good, doctrinal teaching.

In order to meet the challenges of the twenty-first century, preaching must be theologically informed. We face the same problem that Timothy faced: People are turning away from sound theology. People outside the church prefer what novelist David Brooks has termed "flexidoxy," or flexible orthodoxy.[4] In response, we must apply the same remedy that Paul recommended to Timothy: Preach sound doctrine. This is especially important at a time when most people (including many church-goers) have never been introduced to the basic principles of Christian theology. In these post-Christian times, a major pastoral task is to explain Christianity to people who really have no idea what it means. And once people come to Christ, they need to be taught the basic doctrines that will help them think and act the way a Christian should.

It would be a mistake to think that doctrinal preaching is something different from evangelical preaching. The New Testament makes little or no distinction between teaching and evangelism. The apostles understood that the gospel is for Christians as well as non-Christians. Thus their teaching was always evangelistic and their evangelism included a heavy dose of teaching. In keeping with their example, Christian preaching for post-Christian times must be squarely doctrinal as well as solidly evangelical. There can be no preaching for conversion without an announcement of Christ's divine person and saving work, both of which need to be explained in clear doctrinal terms. Similarly, no aspect of Christian theology should ever be taught apart from its relationship to Jesus Christ. And when theological instruction is Christ-centered, it has the power to draw people to salvation in Him.

Preaching must also be *practical,* and this was Paul's primary concern for Timothy. The eternal truths of Scripture must be applied to contemporary culture and to the needs of daily life. To that end, Paul reminded Timothy to be practical in his preaching. A good sermon serves to "correct, rebuke and encourage" (2 Tim. 4:2). To *correct* is to reprove; it is to warn those who persist in sin. To *rebuke* is to censure those who are in error, especially theological error. Here again there is a dual emphasis on life and doctrine. The preacher has a responsibility to teach the Scriptures in a way that reforms belief and transforms conduct. Then to *encourage* is to exhort, to press the truth of Scripture home to the heart. Biblical teaching is not effectively applied unless it comes with life-changing persuasion. Correcting, rebuking, encouraging—these are not the only ways to apply a sermon, but together they remind us that good preaching is as practical as it is evangelical and doctrinal.

THE GREAT NEED FOR BIBLE EXPOSITION

There is more than one way to preach a sermon. It is not my intention to say that every minister must preach exactly the same way on every occasion. The sermons we read in the Bible show that different preaching contexts call for somewhat different sermons. But if faithful preaching includes these three elements—gospel presentation, theological explanation, and practical application—then not just any sermon will do. A minister who wants to preach in the biblical way will not spend all his time preaching revival sermons, such as an evangelist might preach at a rally. Such sermons would be evangelical, but not very doctrinal. He will not deliver theological lectures, such as a scholar might deliver at a seminary. Although such lectures presumably would be doctrinal, they would not be practical. Nor will a minister preach about his own spiritual experience every week, which could be practical, but might not be biblical.

If the church needs evangelical, doctrinal, practical preaching, then the kind of sermon that best satisfies the need is an *expository* sermon. The most effective way to keep Paul's charge to preach the Word is through biblical exposition, the careful and thorough communication of what the Bible actually says. *Thus a Christian church for post-Christian times upholds a tradition of strong expository preaching by gifted men of God.*

Expository preaching means making God's Word plain. In an expository sermon the preacher simply tries to explain what the Bible teaches. The main points of his sermon are the points made by a particular text in the Bible. The minister not only begins with Scripture, but also allows the Scripture to establish the context and content for his entire sermon. The way he decides what to say is by studying what the Bible has to say, so that the Scripture itself sets the agenda for his interpretation and application.

This kind of preaching is most helpfully done when a minister follows the logic of the Scriptures, systematically preaching chapter by chapter and verse by verse through entire books of the Bible. This helps ensure that a congregation hears what God wants them to hear, and not simply what their minister thinks they ought to hear.

But expository preaching is not so much a method as it is a mind-set. A minister who sees himself as an expositor knows that he is not the master of the Word, but its servant. He has no other ambition than to preach what the Scriptures actually teach. His aim is to be faithful to God's Word so that his people can hear God's voice. He himself is only God's mouthpiece, speaking God's message into the ears of God's people, and thus into their minds and hearts. To that end, he carefully works his way through the Scriptures, reading, explaining, and applying them to his congregation. On occasion he may find it necessary to address some pastoral concerns in a topical fashion, but even then his sermons come from his exposition of particular passages of Scripture. Rather than focusing on his own spiritual experience, or on current events, or on what he perceives as his congregation's needs and interests, the minister gives his fullest attention to teaching what the Bible actually says.

During the Protestant Reformation John Calvin made a claim that we can only pray to make about evangelical churches in the twenty-first century. He said: "It is certain that if we come to church we shall not hear only a mortal man speaking but we shall feel (even by his secret power) that God is speaking to our souls, that he is the teacher. He so touches us that the human voice enters into us and so profits us that we are refreshed and nourished by it. God calls us to him as if he had his mouth open and we saw him there in person."[5] And God most clearly speaks this way through a sermon if it is expository—that is, if it makes God's Word plain.

Expository preaching is able to do all the things that good preaching is supposed to do. This is because in expository preaching the minister preaches God's Word. We noted earlier that the whole Bible is about Christ. Therefore, when the Bible is preached, Christ is preached, and sinners are saved. As long as he is careful to preach Christ from all the Scriptures, an expository preacher is an *evangelical* preacher.

He is also a *doctrinal* preacher. All true and sound theology comes from the Word of God. A good expository preacher is careful to explain the doctrines that are taught in each passage of Scripture. As he preaches the Word, therefore, he is preaching biblical theology. Furthermore, he is preaching Christian doctrine in its biblical arrangement and according to its biblical proportions. In many cases, his listeners will be unfamiliar with theological terms and concepts. But this is one of the reasons they need a preacher: to teach them what they need to know about God and His way of salvation.

Expository preaching is also *practical,* which is precisely why Paul told Timothy to preach the Word. The Bible is the most practical book ever written. As Paul understood, practical preaching is biblical preaching—and the more biblical it is, the more practical. God's Word is "useful for teaching, rebuking, correcting and training in righteousness" (2 Tim. 3:16). If that is what the Bible is good for, then it should be used for that purpose. So Paul told Timothy to "correct, rebuke and encourage" (2 Tim. 4:2b). It is astonishing how many personal problems can be resolved when someone hears even a few months of solid expository preaching. Of course, sometimes there is a need for personal counsel, for the private ministry of God's Word. But over time, good expository preaching—in which a minister is careful to draw out the practical implications of the biblical text—addresses the vast majority of spiritual needs. Expository preaching works. This is not the main reason to do it, of course. The reason to preach expository sermons is because it is right. But because it is right, it also works.

THE FINAL ANALYSIS

Expository preaching may seem rather old-fashioned. This is an age of dialogue, and it is often said that preaching needs to become less dogmatic, more conversational. People want the minister to share, not preach. We are also told that Bible exposition is out of place in the information age. People need more stories and fewer propositions. They want preachers to be more personal, less doctrinal.

There are many reasons to be cautious about this kind of thinking. For one thing, information technology has its limitations as well as its strengths. Furthermore, few things are more powerful and persuasive than a living voice preaching a living Word. The personal proclamation of God and His gospel will never become obsolete.

Here it helps to know a little church history, because wherever systematic expository preaching has been practiced, it has brought great blessing to the church. The technical term for this method is *lectio continua*, the reading and teaching of consecutive passages of Scripture. One notable example is John Chrysostom, the great preacher of the fourth century, who transformed the city of Constantinople by expounding large sections of the Bible, especially from the New Testament. Or consider Ulrich Zwingli and John Calvin, who reformed the church primarily through their daily expositions of God's Word. There are more recent examples as well. From his pulpit in Aberdeen, William Still influenced an entire generation of Scottish ministers by preaching and teaching through the entire Bible in fifty years. And here in America the late James Montgomery Boice inspired many men to become better preachers by publishing substantial expositional commentaries on Genesis, Psalms, John, Romans, and many other books of the Bible. The point is that systematic Bible exposition is always beneficial in life-changing and culture-transforming ways. And it will remain beneficial as long as there are sinners who need to be saved and sanctified.

The best reason to practice expository preaching is not simply that it works, however, but that it brings glory to God, which ought to be the ultimate purpose for everything we do. Expository preaching does this by making it clear that all spiritual blessing comes from God's Word, and not from any human being. When a church grows through the plain teaching of God's Word, it becomes obvious that whatever has been accomplished is not due to the gifts of men, but to the grace of God, who alone deserves all the glory.

The apostle Paul was well aware that preaching would not always be popular. This reality seems to lie behind his exhortation to "be prepared in season and out of season" (2 Tim. 4:2). Usually this is taken as a comment on Timothy's own personal circumstances. Whether it is convenient for him or not, he must always be ready to preach at a moment's notice. However, the word for "season" (*kairos*) more properly refers to the times in which he lived. Sometimes preaching seems to be in season; at other times it is out of season, according to popular opinion. But whether it is in season or out of season, Bible exposition is the minister's God-given responsibility, and he must keep doing what God has told him to do. Preaching is God's primary and permanent method for converting sinners and teaching them to grow in grace.

It is an awesome responsibility to preach to the glory of God. Consider the charge Paul gave to Timothy: "In the presence of God and of Christ Jesus, who will judge the living and the dead, and in view of his appearing and his kingdom . . . preach the Word" (2 Tim. 4:1). This is a solemn charge, urgently given with a view to Christ's Second Coming. This is why a calling to pastoral ministry is such serious business. It is a matter of spiritual life and death. It also explains why it is such a serious error for ministers to abandon their responsibility to preach the Bible. In the final analysis, God will hold us accountable for making God's Word plain.

On the day of judgment preachers will not be asked where

they went to seminary or whether they earned any advanced degrees. They will not need to present membership statistics or submit their annual budgets. It will not matter how popular they were or whether they could make people laugh. Instead, when they stand before the heavenly tribunal they will be asked, "Did you preach the Word?" Those who followed their own agenda—or even worse, the world's agenda—will hang their heads in shame. But many humble preachers, who were held in little esteem, will shine in the brightness of their Father's glory. For in their proclamation of God's Word they were faithful to the very end. Their preaching was evangelical, doctrinal, and practical. Their Lord will say to them, "Well done, good and faithful servant! . . . Come and share your master's happiness!" (Matt. 25:23).

3

Giving
Praise to God

Corporate Worship

> *"Come, lift your voice to heaven's high throne,
> and glory give to God alone!"*
>
> —◦ JAMES MONTGOMERY BOICE

Two Americans went to Paris. Since they attended a church back home that met in a shopping mall and featured contemporary worship, what impressed them most was the Cathedral of Notre Dame. As they walked through that grand building and admired its architecture, they stopped in front of the magnificent rose window. As they gazed at the beautiful stained glass, one of them whispered, with some amazement, "Just imagine singing praise choruses in this place. But where do you suppose they put the screen for the overheads?"

This scene first appeared as a cartoon in an evangelical magazine. To appreciate its humor, one probably has to be a veteran of the worship wars. Of all the practical and theological issues that confronted the evangelical church at the end of the twentieth century, among the most divisive was style of worship. While some Christians fought to maintain traditional liturgical forms, others wanted to be more contemporary, and still others tried to be both at the same time ("blended worship," it was called). So evangelicals discussed the relative merits of pipe organs and drum sets. They debated whether the minister should preach from behind a pulpit or atop a bar stool. They tried to figure out whether Scripture songs from the early 1970s still counted as "contemporary" music. And, as in all wars, there were casualties. Some Christians struggled to find churches that had "what they were looking for" in terms of worship style. And in some cases, congregations split in two as members decided to worship their own separate ways. Finally, after all the fighting, *Christianity Today* devoted an issue to the "Triumph of the Praise Songs," seeking to explain "how guitars beat out the organ in the worship wars."[1]

Wars generally have a cause, so it is worth asking what started the worship wars. Was it a matter of spiritual maturity? Did it have something to do with the generation gap? Was it about outreach and evangelism? Was it simply a matter of style —of musical taste—or was there something deeper at work?

SONG OF MYSELF

The way Christians worship is always influenced by the surrounding culture. In these post-Christian times, relativism affects our view of truth and of God, like the Internet executive who said, "I believe in God, but each person has to define that on their own." It is not surprising that in the culture that invented the salad bar and do-it-yourself furniture, people now believe in defining their own deity.

Narcissism, or self-love, also gets plenty of support in a post-Christian culture. Educators and advertisers constantly pro-

mote self-help, self-esteem, self-improvement, self-actualization
—anything and everything having to do with the self. We are
living in relativistic and narcissistic times, when there is no place
for truth, but there is always more room for me.

What happens to worship in such a culture? At least two
things. One is that God's Word tends to get ignored. In an age
of relativism, when people are allergic to absolutes, the Bible becomes increasingly irrelevant. People who demand the freedom
to define reality on their own terms have little use for a divinely
ordained perspective on their existence. So we are now suffering
what the brilliant French apologist Jacques Ellul called "the humiliation of the word."[2] When image is everything, public worship gives less and less time to the reading and preaching of
God's Word.

At the same time, the worship service is coming to be
viewed more and more as a form of entertainment, with music
almost serving as a means of marketing. Often there is an exces-
sive use of songs phrased in the first person singular ("I," "me,"
"my"). As a result, some evangelicals inadvertently spend as
much time singing about themselves and what they're doing ("I
just want to praise You," "I lift Your name," etc.) as they do
singing about God.

Although a fondness for being entertained often character-
izes "seeker-sensitive" churches that favor a contemporary style
of worship, it is also a temptation for traditionalists. We all have
our preferences, and we tend to insist on them. As we have seen,
ours is a narcissistic culture, preoccupied with personal pleasure.
There is an exaltation of the experiential in worship. In this
self-centered age, worship is no longer about glorifying God; it
is about satisfying myself, even feeling good about myself. It is
all about me—what I need, what I like, and what I'm getting
out of it. Worshipers go to church saying, "Here we are, entertain us!" By that standard, things like expository preaching and

pastoral prayer seem far too boring and difficult to appeal to the masses.

Of course, there is always an experiential aspect to Christian worship. But this is a result of being in God's presence, and thus it should never be allowed to become our primary focus. Worship is for God and not for some other purpose, however noble. Leander Keck has explained that since worshiping God is an end in itself, "making worship useful destroys it, because this introduces an ulterior motive for praise. And ulterior motives mean manipulation, taking charge of the relationship, thereby turning the relation between Creator and creature upside down."[3] Thus the congregation cannot be sovereign in worship. God is sovereign, and what is important is not even our own personal experience of God, but God Himself. We only find our true satisfaction when we take our delight in the pleasures of God. Perhaps the best model for the proper approach to God in worship is the book of Psalms. Many of the psalms are deeply personal, yet they never lose their dominant focus on God and His great works of creation and redemption.

To summarize, what happens in a relativistic culture is a change of message: God is no longer allowed to speak His authoritative Word. What happens in a narcissistic culture is a change of audience: Worship is not primarily for God's benefit, but for our own. We like having things our way. Self-centeredness has always been a temptation for God's people. What is new is that many church leaders are now saying that what happens in worship *ought* to be governed by what people want, that we should let culture determine our approach to worship. Kent Hughes laments,

> The unspoken but increasingly common assumption of today's Christendom is that worship is primarily for us—to meet our needs. Such worship services are entertainment focused, and the

worshipers are uncommitted spectators who are silently grading the performance. From this perspective preaching becomes a homiletics of consensus—preaching to felt needs—man's conscious agenda instead of God's. Such preaching is always topical and never textual. Biblical information is minimized, and the sermons are short and full of stories. Anything and everything that is suspected of making the marginal attender uncomfortable is removed from the service. . . . This philosophy instills a tragic self-centeredness. That is, everything is judged by how it affects man. This terribly corrupts one's theology.[4]

LETTING THE WORD DWELL RICHLY

It is not unusual for Christians to fight about worship. Some of the bitterest disputes in church history have centered on the public worship of God. This was true in the Middle Ages, when the Eastern and Western church divided over the use of icons. It was true during the Reformation, when some of the biggest controversies concerned the use of the liturgy, the reading and preaching of Scripture, and the celebration of the sacraments.

Disagreements about how to worship always expose fundamental differences in doctrine. Worship wars are never merely cultural; they are always partly theological. As long as worship is regarded simply as a matter of style or taste, the wars will never end. What the church needs today is a theology of worship to guide its practice of worship.

A biblical theology for Christian worship is taught on every page of Scripture, but perhaps the shortest complete definition comes from Paul's letter to the Colossians: "Let the word of Christ dwell in you richly as you teach and admonish one another with all wisdom, and as you sing psalms, hymns and spiritual songs with gratitude in your hearts to God. And whatever you do, whether in word or deed, do it all in the name of the

Lord Jesus, giving thanks to God the Father through him" (Col. 3:16–17). Although these verses also have wider implications, they help set the parameters for the proper worship of God: The content of worship comes from the Bible, the goal of worship is to give praise to God, and the basis for worship is the saving work of Jesus Christ. Put more simply, true Christian worship is Word-communicating, God-glorifying, and Christ-confessing.

Like everything else in the church, a sound theology of worship begins with the Bible, here identified as "the word of Christ." Although Jesus Christ is the Word incarnate, this phrase refers more specifically to the words that Jesus spoke, to the teaching He gave the apostles, now recorded in the New Testament. The phrase also refers to the gospel of Jesus Christ, which is the message of salvation through the cross and the empty tomb. More generally, it includes the entire Bible, which from beginning to end is all about salvation in Christ.

We are instructed to let the word of Christ dwell in us "richly," that is, "abundantly." This means that the Bible must penetrate deeply into our minds and hearts, which it can only do if we read, study, memorize, teach, hear, and obey it. For God's Word to have its proper effect, we must "receive it with faith and love, lay it up in our hearts, and practice it in our lives."[5] In other words, we must allow God's Word to have its way with us. This is true individually. As we read and study the Bible, we invite the Holy Spirit to instruct our minds and transform our hearts. It should also be true corporately, which is what Paul primarily has in mind here. God wants His Word to have a living presence throughout the church, especially in our worship.

What is the role of the Bible in public worship? First, the various elements of worship are explicitly commanded by Scripture. According to what is sometimes called "the regulative principle for worship," we are not allowed to worship any way we please, but only the way that God pleases. It is not enough to worship the right God; we must also worship Him in the right way, and that means worshiping Him as He has prescribed in His Word. As the Reformers put it, worship must be "according to Scripture."[6] And according to Scripture, the primary elements of worship are praying, reading and preaching God's Word, singing praises, administering the sacraments, and presenting tithes and offerings. In His Word God has reserved a place for each of these activities in public worship.

Not only are these elements of worship prescribed in God's Word, but each of them must be permeated by God's Word. This is obviously true for the reading and preaching of holy Scripture. As Paul said to the Colossians, "Let the word of Christ dwell in you richly as you teach and admonish one another with all wisdom" (Col. 3:16a). Here the words "teach" and "admonish" refer to the proclamation and application of Christian doctrine (see also Col. 1:28). As we saw in the previous chapter, effective Christian preaching is always biblical, doctrinal, and practical. Prayer is also "according to Scripture," for the Bible contains the best models for intercession. Whenever prayer is offered in public worship (whether it is invocation, confession, intercession, thanksgiving, or supplication), it should be graced with the language and phrasing of Scripture. Likewise, the sacraments are governed by God's Word. Baptism and the Lord's Supper are visible words, but in order to celebrate and understand them, we need the teaching of Scripture, including the institution of these sacraments by the Lord Jesus Christ.

What Christians sometimes forget is that the same principle also holds true for worship music. Like everything else in a worship service, the singing of the congregation (and choir) is a Word-communicating activity. Paul plainly states this in

Colossians 3:16. There are several ways to analyze the structure of this verse, but no matter how its grammar is organized, the word of Christ is connected with the praise of God: "Let the word of Christ dwell in you richly . . . as you sing psalms, hymns and spiritual songs with gratitude in your hearts to God" (Col. 3:16; cf. 1 Cor. 14:26; Eph. 5:19–20). One function of church music is didactic; it teaches God's Word in a way that edifies God's people.

Here Paul mentions three different kinds of lyrics: psalms, hymns, and spiritual songs. Scholars have tried to determine what each term means. Some say they all mean essentially the same thing. Others think they refer to three different types of psalms, but it is more likely that only the first word refers to the Old Testament book of Psalms. The word "hymns" seems to refer to Christian hymns, some of which are scattered throughout the New Testament. Then perhaps "spiritual songs" are extemporaneous praises inspired by the Holy Spirit.

Although it is impossible to know exactly what kinds of music Paul had in mind, what is certain is that all our singing must be scriptural. The Bible serves as the primary criterion for songs of praise. The words we sing must be biblically and theologically sound, and the music must serve to reinforce their meaning. One of the theologians who understood this principle best was Martin Luther, who loved to say that "God has preached His gospel through music, too."[7] For Luther, the ministry of music served the ministry of God's Word. He wrote:

> Music and notes, which are wonderful gifts and creations of God, do help gain a better understanding of the text. . . . We have put this music to the living and holy Word of God in order to sing, praise and honor it. We want the beautiful art of music to be properly used to serve her dear Creator and his Christians. He is thereby praised and honored and we are made better and

stronger in faith when his holy Word is impressed on our hearts by sweet music.[8]

Like preaching, the ministry of music is a ministry of the Word. Although all good music has an entertaining quality, its primary function is not to entertain, but to glorify God, and, as it does so, to teach. This has profound implications for the way church musicians should prepare and present their music. The best psalms, hymns, and spiritual songs—whether ancient or modern—enable God's Word to dwell in us *richly*. This should be true of all our worship. Whenever we worship in the biblical way we are communicating God's Word, because every element of our worship is both prescribed in and permeated by Scripture.

GLORIFYING GOD IN OUR HEARTS

Worship not only edifies, but it also glorifies. This brings us to the goal of worship, which is the glory of God. Our worship is logocentric—it communicates God's Word. At the same time, it is also *theocentric*—it gives praise to God. In fact, it is just because worship is logocentric that it is theocentric (and vice versa). Worship is all about God because it is directed by His very own Word.

Twice in chapter 3 Paul reminded the Colossians to glorify God in their worship, first in verse 16 ("with gratitude in your hearts to God"), and then again in verse 17 ("giving thanks to God the Father through him"). His point is so obvious that it hardly needs to be explained: The whole purpose of worship— and, indeed, of human existence—is to give glory to God. In fact, this is what the word "worship" means. It comes from the old Anglo-Saxon term "worth-ship." This is exactly what worship is: giving honor to God for His supremacy, and thereby acknowledging His genuine worth. True worship is doxological; it gives praise to God.

It is right for God to receive all the praise. It is right because of who He is. God—and God alone—has all wisdom, knowledge, power, and strength. He is the perfectly and infinitely loving, holy, just, merciful, and faithful God. It is also right for Him to receive all the praise because of what He has done. God—and God alone—made the whole universe out of nothing. He alone sustains the cosmos by the word of His power and preserves and governs all His creatures. And God alone has saved His people from their sins. God chose us, called us, justified us, and adopted us. Right now He is sanctifying us, and one day He will glorify us. From creation to redemption, God deserves all the glory for all eternity. This explains why in the entire Bible not one single word of worship is wasted on any other deity, but glory is given to God alone—Father, Son, and Holy Spirit. Only God deserves the glory, and to the extent that our worship is not thoroughly God-centered, it is blasphemous.

We need to be reminded of this because post-Christian culture is not theocentric (God-centered), but egocentric (self-centered), and thus we are in constant danger of forgetting whom we have come to worship. Gene Edward Veith, a Lutheran scholar and a keen observer of Christianity and culture, writes:

> Entertainment is not the purpose for going to church. Indulging ourselves in aesthetic pleasure is not the same as worshiping. Churches dare not choreograph their worship services to add entertainment value, even to attract nonbelievers. . . . To do so in worship . . . risks undercutting the Christian message. Ours is a culture wholly centered upon the self. The church must counter this egotism, not give in to it. The Bible calls us to repentance, faith, service, and self-denial—qualities utterly opposed to the entertainment mentality. In Christian worship, the congregation is not the audience; God is the audience.[9]

Theologian Donald Bloesch writes in a similar vein, lamenting the current state of Christian worship:

> Our worship is essentially a spectacle that appeals to the senses rather than an act of obeisance to the mighty God who is both holiness and love. Contemporary worship is far more egocentric than theocentric. The aim is less to give glory to God than to satisfy the longings of the human heart. Even when we sing God's praises, the focus is on fulfilling and satisfying the human desire for wholeness and serenity. This motivation is not wrong in itself but becomes questionable when it takes priority.[10]

These warnings apply every bit as much to traditional worship as they do to contemporary worship. The danger is especially acute with worship music because music is frequently used in our culture for the purpose of entertainment. But whether the appetite for entertainment comes from the concert hall or the sound studio, the problem is the same, namely, turning praise into a performance (and receiving it as such).

When we worship, we constantly have to remind ourselves who the audience is. In the twenty-first century the church may be the only place where our attention is turned away from ourselves and back to God. A popular Christian T-shirt rightly claims, "It's not about me." Implication: It's all about Christ. What Christians say to a post-Christian culture is "It's not about you, either; it's all about God." The way to say this is by giving praise to the living God, and especially by preserving a sense of the sacred in public worship. In a self-centered culture, nothing is more countercultural than transcendent, God-centered worship.

This principle—that worship is for God and His glory—has several implications. One is that true worship demands everything we have. Paul told the Colossians to worship with "gratitude in [their] hearts to God" (Col. 3:16). When he said "hearts," he did not mean that worship was primarily a matter of feeling the right way about God. Rather, he was saying that true worship must be inward as well as outward. The heart is the center of a person's whole being. So when the Bible tells us to worship God in our hearts, what it really means is to worship God with everything we are and everything we have—to love Him with mind, soul, body, and spirit. Marva Dawn writes, "The biblical word *heart* signifies the wholistic will, not merely the emotions, and thus emphasizes that we worship God intentionally, deliberately, mindfully—even when we don't feel like it—since God is worthy of our adoration."[11]

People sometimes wonder what kind of music God likes. The answer is music that comes from our whole person. No matter how biblical and orthodox the content of our music, and no matter how skillfully we sing or play, what we offer God in worship only pleases Him if it comes from our whole person. In worship what is more important than style is sanctity—the worshiper setting God apart as sacred. The New Testament thus describes our worship as a "sacrifice" in which we unreservedly offer our whole selves up to God (Rom. 12:1; Heb. 13:15).

Another implication of glorifying God as the goal of our worship is that in order to please God we must worship Him with excellence. The God we seek to glorify has created a world in which there are real artistic standards. What kind of music does God like? Excellent music. Our worship music must be appropriate to His character. Thus the excellence of His divine being establishes the criteria for our worship.

The need for excellence obviously has special importance for musicians. The Bible mentions a wide variety of instruments that are suitable for public worship, including strings, woodwinds, brass, and percussion. It does not seem to prefer any one instrument over the others. Depending on the words to be sung, some instruments may be more appropriate than others. The music needs to match the message. But one thing the Bible does insist is that whatever instruments are used must be played with real musical excellence: "Sing joyfully to the LORD, you righteous. . . . Sing to him a new song; play skillfully, and shout for joy" (Ps. 33:1a, 3). This implies that a church should employ the talents of its very best musicians. Furthermore, the music they play should itself be excellent. Its melodies and harmonies should display beauty, intricacy, and all the other qualities that make for great music. A hymn or song can be musically inferior even if its text is biblically acceptable. Having this concern for the quality of worship music need not be a form of elitism. It is simply a commitment to excellence, based on the fact that God is the audience, and He always demands our very best.

A further implication of glorifying God in our worship concerns evangelism. Worship is not primarily for the benefit of non-Christians. Some churches choose their worship music on the basis of what they think will appeal to outsiders. However, although effective evangelism can occur in worship, the purpose of a worship service is not primarily evangelistic. This is commonly misunderstood. As Marva Dawn has observed, some worship leaders "confuse worship with evangelism and evangelism with marketing."[12] Certainly a church should do what it can to make visitors feel welcome and to help people understand what is happening in the worship service. In order to fulfill its Word-communicating function, Christian worship must be intelligible even if it can never be completely accessible to the unconverted. It is also appropriate for churches to hold services with a special evangelistic focus. However, a twenty-first-century church must never forget that since worship is for the glory of God, other people are not the audience. Worship is for God, not for unbelievers.

It is only when we remember to give praise to God that our worship is able to do its gospel work. In his first letter to the

Corinthians, the apostle Paul imagines an unbeliever getting converted during a worship service. What convinced the man to become a Christian? It was not because he felt comfortable. It was not because he liked the music. It was not because he felt like he could relate to the worship service. No, it was the preaching of God's Word, in a context where all the glory was given to God. Paul wrote, "If an unbeliever or someone who does not understand comes in while everybody is prophesying, he will be convinced by all that he is a sinner and will be judged by all, and the secrets of his heart will be laid bare. So he will fall down and worship God, exclaiming, 'God is really among you!'" (1 Cor. 14:24–25). The man did not come to faith because he was in a familiar environment, but because he was confronted with a whole new spiritual reality.

What makes a church most effective in evangelism is God's living presence in its worship. But this requires the whole congregation to acknowledge His presence by exalting His transcendence and reveling in His grace. One of the ways a Christian church for post-Christian times spreads the gospel is by glorifying God as a worshiping community. Presumably visitors will not understand everything that transpires during a worship service. Nor will they be able truly to worship God until their lives are regenerated by His Spirit. But when God is worshiped in true splendor and majesty, they will be compelled to say, "Wow! God is really here!"

Doing it All in Jesus' Name

There is one major difficulty with God-centered worship: God is dangerous, and thus it is not altogether safe to come into His presence. Just ask Moses. Or Nadab and Abihu. Or Uzzah. Or Isaiah. Or Job. Or Ananias and Sapphira. All of these people had close encounters with the God of glory. In some cases they were utterly destroyed by the terror of His majesty. In other cases they were simply undone by the brightness of His glory. But in every case they discovered that it is not completely safe to worship a God who is glorious in His holiness.

It is for this reason that we give praise to God *in Jesus' name*. Our worship must be Christ-honoring. As Paul told the Colossians: "And whatever you do, whether in word or deed, do it all in the name of the Lord Jesus, giving thanks to God the Father through him" (Col. 3:17; cf. Eph. 5:20). This verse is for the whole Christian life. Everything we do should be done in Jesus' name, and for God's greater glory. But this principle has special relevance for corporate worship, when we worship in Jesus' name.

God's name is never simply a title, but it always represents the full majesty of His being and attributes. The name of Jesus refers specifically to His person and work as the Savior of sinners. It is the name of salvation. So, for example, when Peter preached about Christ's saving work, he said, "Salvation is found in no one else, for there is no other name under heaven given to men by which we must be saved" (Acts 4:12; cf. Rom. 10:13). Those who "believe in the name" of Jesus have eternal life (1 John 5:13). Then they are baptized in Jesus' name (Acts 10:48). And when Paul wanted to remind the Corinthians how far they had come in the Christian life, he said, "You were justified in the name of the Lord Jesus Christ" (1 Cor. 6:11). All of salvation and the whole Christian life fall under the name of the Lord Jesus. When we say "in Jesus' name," therefore, it is not an afterthought (or at least it shouldn't be), but it expresses full salvation in Jesus Christ.

Whenever Christians gather for worship—even in twos and threes—they meet in Jesus' name (Matt. 18:20). What does it mean to give thanks to God in and through "the name of the Lord Jesus"? To worship in Jesus' name means to worship God on the basis of Christ's sufferings and death. In this connection it is worth noting that the phrase "with gratitude" can also be translated "in the grace," meaning the grace that God has given through Jesus Christ. It is only on the basis of Christ's atoning work that anyone can ever approach God. Before we can approach God in worship, we must be reconciled to Him through Christ and His cross. "Once you were alienated from God," Paul reminded the Colossians, "and were enemies in your minds because of your evil behavior. But now he has reconciled you by Christ's physical body through death to present you holy in his sight, without blemish and free from accusation" (Col. 1:21–22).

In these post-Christian times, some people deny our need for such atonement. According to one theologian, Christianity must be liberated from "an abusive theology that glorifies suffering. . . . We must do away with the atonement, this idea of a blood sin upon the whole human race that can be washed away only by the blood of the lamb. . . . We do not need to be saved by Jesus' death from some original sin."[13] But of course that is exactly what we *do* need: Christ's work on the cross, His sufferings and death in the place of sinners. We need His atoning work for many reasons, not least because we cannot worship without it. Worship that is pleasing to God is worship that honors Jesus Christ, without whom it is impossible to worship God at all (Heb. 10:19–22).

If we are to please God in our worship, then, our worship must be Word-communicating, God-glorifying, and Christ-honoring. A great deal more could be said about how to apply these principles, but having the right theology of worship will help us please God in our practice of worship. Does our worship communicate the right content, which is the Word of God? Are we pursuing the right goal, which is to glorify God? Are we coming on the right basis, which is the saving work of Jesus Christ?

If the answer to these questions is yes, then we will be able to do what a church must do in these post-Christian times: *Worship God in a worthy manner through thoughtful words, devoted prayers, and excellent music.* This is precisely what our culture needs, for the answer to relativism is God's true Word and the answer to narcissism is God-centered worship. So let the word of Christ dwell in you richly as you give thanks to God the Father through the Lord Jesus!

4

Growing
Together in Groups

✝

Fellowship

> *"We must uphold a familiar commerce together in all meekness, gentleness, patience and liberality, we must delight in each other, make others' conditions our own, rejoice together, mourn together, labor and suffer together, always having before our eyes . . . our community as members of the same body."*
>
> —⌁ JOHN WINTHROP

A re *you* the stranger who will rescue me?" This is the question Andy asks in Douglas Coupland's influential book, *Generation X: Tales for an Accelerated Culture.* Whenever Andy meets someone new, his unspoken question is, "Are *you* the stranger who will rescue me?"[1]

As Andy's question suggests, Coupland's novel is about the search for identity and community in the information age. *Generation X* defines the aspirations of America's first postmodern generation, in which people desperately want to know who they are and where they belong, yet have trouble finding the answers. When truth is relative, it becomes difficult to establish a fixed identity, as the "X" in "Generation X" implies. Personal identity is not a given, but a variable—a blank that is still waiting to be filled in. When this uncertainty is combined with narcissism, or radical self-centeredness, it becomes nearly impossible to build a caring community.

Generation X identifies two attitudes, common among young Americans, that contribute to the present crisis of community. One is the "Cult of Aloneness," which Coupland defines as "the need for autonomy at all costs, usually at the expense of long-term relationships. Often brought about by overly high expectations of others."[2] At the same time, the next generation suffers from what Coupland calls "Terminal Wanderlust: A condition common to people of transient middle-class upbringings. Unable to feel rooted in any one environment, they move continually in the hopes of finding an idealized sense of community in the next location."[3] It is not hard to see how these two attitudes are related. The cult of aloneness is one form of narcissism. It insists on individual autonomy without interpersonal responsibility, which of course makes authentic community impossible. Yet human beings are made for community, so the next generation keeps looking for a place to belong. Hence its terminal wanderlust.

What can help the next generation clarify its identity? Where can it find the caring community it craves? Not from the government, because Generation X is cynical about political authority. Not in the marketplace, because most young workers will change careers more than five times before they retire. Not even at home, because the next generation has watched the American family implode, and thus it is pessimistic about combining love with commitment. Coupland's book ends with a series of depressing statistics about American family life, followed by this haunting question: "Would you like to have a marriage like the one your parents had?"[4]

BODY LIFE

What the next generation needs is what every generation needs: the kind of caring community that can only be found in the church of Jesus Christ. This book began with the claim that a Christian church for post-Christian times must be a teaching, worshiping, and caring church, much like the one the apostles established in the first century. In chapter 2 we saw that a teaching church preaches God's Word in an evangelical, doctrinal, and practical way. Chapter 3 was about worship—giving praise to God in a God-glorifying, Word-communicating, and Christ-honoring way. In this chapter we turn our attention to caring, to the life of love that God has given us to share in the church of Jesus Christ.

Teaching, worshiping, caring—this is the proper order. First God reaches down to us, forgiving our sins through the gospel of Jesus Christ. That is the saving message we teach and preach. As soon as we come to faith in Christ, we start to give praise to God for the gift of His grace, turning our faces up to Him in worship. The Christian community is formed around the Word and the worship of God. But God has also commanded us to love one another, so we must reach outward as well as upward, turning to one another in care and compassion. When we lower our gaze from worshiping God, the first thing we see is another human being—probably someone who needs our help.

The New Testament uses a variety of metaphors to describe caring Christian community, or what theologians call "the communion of saints." The church is a building in which each Christian is a living stone (I Pet. 2:4–5). Or, to get rid of the masonry for a moment, the church is God's household (Eph. 2:19), a spiritual family. Christians are also called citizens of God's great city. But the most common metaphor compares the church to a body: "You are the body of Christ, and each one of you is a part of it" (I Cor. 12:27; cf. Rom. 12:4–8; Eph. 1:22–23; 4:12; Col. 1:24).

The identity of the church as the body of Christ is most carefully worked out in I Corinthians 12. The main point of this chapter is that there is one and only one body of Christ: "The body is a unit, though it is made up of many parts; and though all its parts are many, they form one body. So it is with Christ" (I Cor. 12:12). Or again, according to the climactic verse of the passage, "You are the body of Christ, and each one of you is a part of it" (I Cor. 12:27).

The body of Christ includes everyone who is connected to Jesus Christ by faith. How does someone become part of this body? Through baptism, "For we were all baptized by one Spirit into one body" (I Cor. 12:13a; cf. Gal. 3:27). Scholars debate whether baptism here refers to water baptism or to some kind of spiritual baptism. Possibly both are in view. Certainly we are joined to the body of Christ as soon as we are born again by God's Spirit. But the outward sign of belonging to His body is water baptism. This shows the vital importance of baptism in post-Christian times. We belong to the body of Christ, and what places us in that alternative community is the sacrament of baptism. Baptism is a countercultural act, almost a form of protest. Over against everything else that tries to define us—our career, our citizenship, our status as consumers in a market economy—baptism locates our primary identity in the body of Christ, specifically as members of a local church. We are not defined by what we do, where we live, or what we buy. We are defined by our relationship to God, who by His Spirit has joined us to the body of Christ.

Belonging to the church not only answers the question of our identity, but it also satisfies our need for community. People are asking, "Who am I? Where do I belong?" For the Christian, the answer is "I belong to the body of Christ, of which I am a member." Christianity has never been a private religion. It is personal, of course, because it involves a personal relationship with Jesus Christ, the crucified and risen Savior. But in coming to Christ, who is the head of the body, every single Christian gets connected to every other Christian. Our union with Christ brings us into communion with His church as members of a local congregation.

In the past, the evangelical church has emphasized the need to make a personal commitment to Jesus Christ. But this cannot be separated from making a public commitment to His church. In his book *The Body,* Charles Colson writes:

> Serious Christians know they need discipleship; they want to be faithful and to make a difference. But the fact is, even Christians who understand their personal identity as followers of Christ will not make a widespread difference in the decline and decay around us—unless we have a high view of our corporate identity as the body of Christ. . . . Christianity is not a solitary belief system. Any genuine resurgence of Christianity, as history demonstrates, depends on a reawakening and renewal of that which is the essence of the faith—that is, the people of God, the new society, the body of Christ, which is made manifest in the world—the Church . . . there is no such thing as Christianity apart from the Church.[5]

What is remarkable is that in order to establish this new spiritual society, the church crosses almost every other social boundary. This is a fact Paul emphasizes: "For we were all baptized by one Spirit into one body—whether Jews or Greeks, slave or free" (I Cor. 12:13; cf. Gal. 3:28). Here the apostle refers to what are always two of the biggest barriers to social harmony: ethnicity and economics. Division by race and class hinders every attempt to establish human community. There are other barriers as well—for example, gender differences exacerbated by the battle of the sexes, social differences caused by physical handicaps, generational differences caused by a gap in ages.

The result of all these barriers is that in these post-Christian times, America is a deeply divided country, characterized by alienation, isolation, and segregation. Surprising evidence for this comes from the 2000 U.S. Census, which revealed that although our country is becoming more and more ethnically diverse, our communities remain as segregated as ever, if not more so. One analyst concluded that "four decades of efforts to integrate communities have largely failed. While other research suggests that racial attitudes with regard to housing have lessened, actual settlement patterns remain rooted in the past. Children of the early 21st century will likely grow up isolated from people of other ethnic groups."[6]

The church is called to be different. Completely different. We belong to Jesus Christ, because we have all been baptized into His body. Now the powerful presence of the Holy Spirit gives us a spiritual unity that overcomes our differences, enabling us to live together in a caring community that stands out like a city on a hill.

One of my greatest joys as a minister is to welcome new members into the fellowship of our church. During Sunday morning worship the new members are introduced, their testimonies are read, and they line up at the front of the sanctuary to take their membership vows. Since we are a diverse urban congregation, it is not unusual for us to receive a wide variety of newcomers: young and old, married and single, black and white, Americans and internationals, able-bodied and disabled, rich and poor. One Sunday as I surveyed the new members, I leaned over to a colleague and said, "You know, there's no other place in the whole world where this group of people would gather for a common purpose." The only thing that can explain this kind of unity is the gracious work of God's Spirit, who makes us one in the body of Christ.

BODY PARTS

As we have seen, one unique thing about the church is its diversity. The Christian community is not homogeneous, but heterogeneous, consisting of all different kinds of people. This is one of the reasons that the analogy of the body is so appropriate, because, like any body, the body of Christ consists of many different parts: "Now the body is not made up of one part but of many" (I Cor. 12:14).

Each body part has its own unique function. So to apply the analogy, every Christian has a specific role in the church. And in order to carry out that role, every member has been given one or more spiritual gifts: "There are different kinds of gifts, but the same Spirit. There are different kinds of service, but the same Lord. There are different kinds of working, but the same God works all of them in all men. Now to each one the manifestation of the Spirit is given for the common good" (I Cor. 12:4–7).

The Holy Spirit has distributed a diversity of spiritual gifts (here also called a "service," a "working," or a "manifestation") throughout the body of Christ. These gifts are essential to Christian community. However, since they are increasingly misunderstood and ignored, this is a good place to answer some basic questions about them.

What is a spiritual gift? Obviously enough, it is a *gift*. In other words, it is something God gives, something He works into the Christian (I Cor. 12:6). The biblical word for gift *(charisma)* is derived from the same root as the biblical word for grace *(charis)*. Both words describe something that comes from God as a gracious gift. To be more specific, these gifts come through God the Holy Spirit, which is why they are called *spiritual* gifts: "All these [gifts] are the work of one and the same Spirit, and he gives them to each one, just as he determines" (1 Cor. 12:11).

What the Spirit gives (ordinarily at the time of conversion) is a special ability that strengthens the church or builds up the body of Christ (Eph. 4:12). Ray Stedman defined a spiritual gift as "a capacity for service which is given to every true Christian without exception and which was something each did not possess before he became a Christian."[7] A spiritual gift, therefore, is not quite the same thing as a natural ability, although the two are sometimes related. Snorkeling is not a spiritual gift. Neither is the ability to hang sheet rock. However, some spiritual gifts can be expressed by using a natural talent. For example, a Christian may exercise the spiritual gift of helping through the natural talent of cooking. Or an aptitude for public speaking may be useful or even necessary for someone who exercises the gift of preaching. What distinguishes a spiritual gift is that it is used for a spiritual purpose in the body of Christ, and thus it has the blessing of God's Spirit.

What kinds of spiritual gifts are available? First Corinthians 12:8–10 provides a fairly complete list. It includes wisdom, knowledge, faith, healing, miracles, prophecy, discernment, tongues, and interpretation. Later Paul adds teaching, helping, and administration (1 Cor. 12:28–30). Other New Testament passages mention service, encouragement, giving, leadership, mercy (all in Rom. 12:6–18), and evangelism (Eph. 4:11). None of these lists is complete, and although there is some overlap, no two lists are exactly the same. God has distributed a wide variety of gifts throughout the body of Christ. As Peter said, "Each one should use whatever gift he has received to serve others, faithfully administering God's grace in its various forms" (1 Pet. 4:10).

If every Christian has at least one spiritual gift to use in the service of Christ, the obvious question is, *How can I identify my gift(s)?* Begin by studying what the Bible has to say about spiritual gifts, what kinds there are, and how they are to be used. As you study, pray that God will help you recognize your spiritual gifts. Then begin to make a sober assessment of your natural talents (Rom. 12:3), asking how the Holy Spirit wants you to use them to glorify God and benefit others. In making this assessment, it is important to seek the counsel of the church, because a true spiritual gift will be evident to other members of the body. Finally, take advantage of opportunities to serve, so that you can begin to evaluate and exercise your gifts. If you are willing to serve, God will show you how.

THE BODY NEEDS YOU

Every member's gift is essential to the health of the body. There are two sides to this: The body needs you, and you need the body. To make this point, the apostle Paul imagines how absurd it would be for a Christian to decide that his or her gifts were no longer needed:

> If the foot should say, "Because I am not a hand, I do not belong to the body," it would not for that reason cease to be part of the body. And if the ear should say, "Because I am not an eye, I do not belong to the body," it would not for that reason cease to be part of the body. If the whole body were an eye, where would the sense of hearing be? If the whole body were an ear, where would the sense of smell be? (1 Cor. 12:15–17)

One imagines an enormous eyeball rolling around the church, or someone trying to smell with a humongous ear!

Paul used this kind of humor because he wanted to show

81

how ridiculous it is for Christians to despise their own spiritual gifts. Every member not only belongs to the body, but is necessary to its health and welfare. There is no appendix in the body of Christ. If you are a Christian, then even if you don't fit in anywhere else, you belong to Christ and His church. Every member is important. No one is superfluous. This means that every Christian has a job to do. The body only functions properly "as each part does its work" (Eph. 4:16). Even Christians who don't think they have much to offer must offer whatever they have. In the words of the Heidelberg Catechism, "Every one must know it to be his duty, readily and cheerfully to employ his gifts for the advantage and salvation of other members" (A. 55).

If it is true that every member is essential, then it is foolish for a Christian to want someone else's ministry. One cartoon depicts a man in an armchair holding a report out to his dog and saying, "Rover, your gift test indicates you'd do best at fetching and sitting at my feet, but our family needs someone to sit on the branches and sing. Do you think you could handle that?" The trouble, of course, is that singing from the treetops doesn't come in the same gift mix with fetching and barking. Yet sadly, some Christians try to carry out a ministry to which they are not called. Usually this is because they think (wrongly and often narcissistically) that they deserve a more prominent position in the church.

Others covet spiritual gifts that God has not given to them. It is significant that the foot envies the hand—a body part that looks similar, but seems more useful because it has special features (such as an opposable thumb). Somehow it is not surprising for the foot to envy the hand. Or for the ear to want to be an eye, for that matter. But of course this is all silly. The body can only function properly if each member plays its own part. To be unhappy with one's gifts is to destroy the very idea of ministry in the church, which depends on a diversity of ability. It is also rebellion against God. A spiritual gift is not something we choose for ourselves; it is something chosen for us, and thus it is to be received with gratitude. If we are discontent with our spiritual gifts, then we are really contending against God, who "has arranged the parts in the body, every one of them, just as he wanted them to be" (I Cor. 12:18; cf. Eph. 4:7). The body of Christ is harmed whenever its members refuse to accept the part that God has given them to play.

YOU NEED THE BODY

It is equally harmful when members are unwilling to accept the role that God has given to others. This is the opposite side of the same problem. Some Christians feel that they are not very important; Paul dealt with this issue in verses 14 to 18 of I Corinthians 12. Others think much too highly of themselves, which he addresses in the verses that follow:

> If they were all one part, where would the body be? As it is, there are many parts, but one body. The eye cannot say to the hand, "I don't need you!" And the head cannot say to the feet, "I don't need you!" On the contrary, those parts of the body that seem to be weaker are indispensable, and the parts that we think are less honorable we treat with special honor. And the parts that are unpresentable are treated with special modesty, while our presentable parts need no special treatment. But God has combined the members of the body and has given greater honor to the parts that lacked it, so that there should be no division in the body, but that its parts should have equal concern for each other. (I Cor. 12:19–25)

As much as the body needs you, you also need the body— every part of it. The wholeness of the body depends on the diversity of its parts. We were baptized by one Spirit into one body of Christ, but in order to live as a body, we depend on one another. The same is true for any body: In order to act in a coordinated way, every part must fulfill its own unique function. Thus the unity of the body of Christ is demonstrated through its diversity. The apostle Paul said the same thing to the Romans: "Just as each of us has one body with many members, and these members do not all have the same function, so in Christ we who are many form one body, and each member belongs to all the others" (Rom. 12:4–5).

The reason Paul emphasizes this is that Christians tend to exaggerate their own importance. In fact, sometimes we are tempted to think that we don't need anyone else, that we are spiritually self-sufficient. But the moment we start to think about how important we are to the body of Christ, it becomes impossible to do any really Christian work at all, because serving Christ is all about serving others: "Nobody should seek his own good, but the good of others" (1 Cor. 10:24). Spiritual gifts are never intended for private use, but are always for the benefit of the whole church. Or as Paul said in 1 Corinthians 12:7, spiritual gifts are given "for the common good." Thus we are mutually interdependent. What is true for the human body is true for the body of Christ: The various parts cannot exist on their own, but they depend on the life of the whole body. To put it very simply, we need each other.

Recognizing our need for others can help us escape our obsession with ourselves. Christopher Lasch concluded in his famous exposé of narcissism in America that our "best hope of emotional maturity" requires

> a recognition of our need for and dependence on people who nevertheless remain separate from ourselves and refuse to submit to our whims. It lies in a recognition of others not as projections

of our own desires but as independent beings with desires of their own. More broadly, it lies in acceptance of our limits. The world does not exist merely to satisfy our own desires.[8]

Although Lasch did not have the church specifically in mind, the body of Christ is the best place to learn how much we need to depend on others. Belonging to the church draws us out of our usual self-centeredness into relationships of mutual love and concern.

In the church we are so interdependent that every spiritual gift makes an essential contribution. Even "those parts of the body that seem to be weaker are indispensable" (1 Cor. 12:22). The word used here for weakness is the Greek word *asthenes*, which means "sickly." Paul is not talking about physical weakness, but spiritual weakness. Some Christians are stronger than others. They are more gifted, or perhaps they have more faith, so that they are able to use their gifts more effectively. But even the gifts of weaker Christians are necessary. This is true in any organization: The general cannot fight unless he has foot soldiers to command; the architect cannot build without bricklayers; the law firm cannot try a case without a team of paralegals.

This principle—that every member is essential—has profound implications for life in the body of Christ. Think of the neediest member in your Bible study, or the church committee member who always opposes your motions, or the person in your ministry who has only one spiritual gift (at the most). Do not look down on that person! He or she belongs to the body of Christ, and, according to God's Word, deserves special honor. If that honor is not given, the church will be divided: "God has combined the members of the body and has given greater honor to the parts that lacked it, so that there should be no division in the body" (1 Cor. 12:24b–25a).

Even the weakest Christian deserves special care. Paul ends

this passage by insisting that the various parts of the body "should have equal concern for each other. If one part suffers, every part suffers with it; if one part is honored, every part rejoices with it" (I Cor. 12:25b–26). These words are filled with passion. The Greek word for concern (*merimnao*) means passionate concern—deep personal care for another Christian. This care and concern is to be expressed in both good times and bad times. It includes helping meet the practical and material needs of other members of the body (see Rom. 12:13; I John 3:17). But it also calls for a deep emotional response to their joys and sorrows. We are called to "suffer with" (*sumpaschei*, from which we get the English word "sympathy") and "rejoice with" one another. A Christian church is a caring community in which we consider what happens to someone else to be every bit as important as what happens to ourselves.

One place I have seen these principles put into practice is within the close fellowship of a Philadelphia Bible study. For years a diverse group of church members met together weekly for prayer and Bible study. Then a woman joined the group who was still learning what it meant to follow Christ. She was extremely needy—spiritually, emotionally, physically, and otherwise. She didn't always understand the Bible, but she kept coming. And she kept being loved. Many weeks the only thing she seemed to contribute were her prayer requests and her questions—basic, sometimes blunt questions about how the gospel really worked in daily life.

The woman had cancer, and, as her illness progressed, members of the group rallied to her aid, learning in the process how to depend more deeply on one another. They took her to the doctor, stopped by to talk, brought her groceries, helped settle her personal affairs, visited her at the hospital, and gathered at her bedside to pray and sing. By the time she died, the woman had received far more than she had given. Or had she?

She was a good friend, with a good sense of humor, and she was generous with her love. The members of her Bible study would say that in her weakness she deserved special honor, and that in addition to everything else, she had given them the greatest gift of all: an opportunity to care.

GETTING INTO GROUPS

The biblical teaching on the body of Christ raises a very practical question: How should we organize church life so that all these things can happen? The Bible tells us to "encourage one another daily" (Heb. 3:13). Obviously, then, it is not enough for us to get together for worship once a week. A church that met only weekly might be a teaching church and a worshiping church, but it could hardly be a caring church.

Here it is important to remember what a fractured, fragmented society we generally live in from Monday to Saturday. As Charles Reich wrote in his best-selling book *The Greening of America:*

> Modern living has obliterated place, locality and neighborhood, and given us the anonymous separateness of our existence. The family, the most basic social system, has been ruthlessly stripped to its functional essentials. Friendship has been coated over with a layer of impenetrable artificiality as men strive to live roles designed for them. Protocol, competition, hostility, and fear have replaced the warmth of the circle of affection which might sustain man against a hostile environment. . . . America [has become] one vast, terrifying anti-community.[9]

In order to overcome these obstacles and to form a functional spiritual community, Christians need to stay connected to the body of Christ all week long. We need regular opportunities to use our spiritual gifts and to profit from the gifts of others. We need to live in close enough community to suffer with those who suffer and rejoice with those who rejoice. And we need to know one another well enough to hold each other accountable for spiritual progress.

It is hard to see how all of this can be accomplished in the body of Christ unless Christians are growing together in smaller groups. Earlier we noted that the church is a spiritual family. In order to function as a family we need smaller gatherings, including some that are closer in size to a nuclear family. *To establish a caring community, a Christian church for post-Christian times integrates every member of the congregation into Bible studies and other groups where individual needs can be met and each can minister to others.*

Many different kinds of groups can accomplish this purpose. Some churches are organized into parishes under the spiritual oversight of elders (more about them in the next chapter). Sunday school classes, midweek prayer meetings, and other forms of Christian education can provide regular opportunities for mutual ministry. There is also a place for affinity groups, in which people in similar life situations meet for mutual encouragement. To that end, churches often establish a youth group, a singles ministry, a men's breakfast, a program for mothers with small children, and so on. Then there are groups that serve within the church, such as ministry teams that collect the offering or organize fellowship events. Beyond that, there is outreach to the surrounding community, which enables Christians to use their spiritual gifts as they form partnerships in servant ministry. A group might lead worship in a local nursing home, conduct a Bible study in a local prison, or prepare food for the homeless. All of these groups can strengthen the common life of Christ's body, and all of them should incorporate Bible teaching, prayer, and fellowship, as appropriate to the context. There is also a place for prayer partners and other one-on-one relationships that promote personal discipleship. But perhaps the best place for ministering to others and meeting individual needs is the small group Bible study.

Small groups are sometimes considered a relatively recent phenomenon. Among evangelicals, home Bible studies became especially popular during and after the 1970s. Yet a closer look at church history shows that meeting in small groups is not a temporary fad, but an ordinary aspect of healthy body life.

The New Testament churches were house groups, not megachurches. In Acts 2 we read that in addition to meeting at the temple for worship, the first Christians broke bread together in their homes. Both the large group that met at the temple and the small group that met in someone's home were called "the church." In his letter to the Romans, the apostle Paul sent greetings to the church that met at the house of Priscilla and Aquila (Rom. 16:5). And when he went to Ephesus, he taught "from house to house" (Acts 20:20). Small groups have flourished throughout the history of the church. At its best, the medieval monastic movement was an attempt to preserve body life in small Christian communities. During the Reformation, local ministers met weekly for prayer and Bible teaching. Many Puritans met in the evenings to encourage one another in spiritual things. John Wesley was converted at a midweek meeting, and wherever he preached, he encouraged Christians to form small groups to study the Bible and to pray. Small groups—in a wide variety of shapes and sizes—have a long and valued history in the church. When we emphasize their importance for post-Christian times, we are really going back to the historical pattern.

What should take place in a small group? Everything the church does is based on God's Word, so the most important thing is to provide sound biblical instruction. A small group is one of the places where the word of Christ is to "dwell in [us] richly as [we] teach and admonish one another with all wisdom"

(Col. 3:16a). Although teaching and admonishing are the special prerogatives of the pastor, to a certain extent this command applies to every Christian. Paul told the Romans that they were "full of goodness, complete in knowledge and competent to instruct one another" (Rom. 15:14). However, not every Christian has the spiritual gift of teaching. One of the advantages of effective small groups is that they provide an opportunity for Christians to think together about practical ways to apply the teaching of Scripture. The problem with some inductive Bible studies, however, is that members end up pooling their ignorance. God has not called Christians simply to "share," but to instruct. So it is essential for small group leaders to be able to teach, and to do so under the spiritual oversight of the church. To provide proper spiritual care and to ensure that instruction is theologically orthodox, every Bible study should be hosted and/or taught by a church member and should be connected—either directly or indirectly—to the spiritual care of the church's ordained leaders. Like every other part of the body of Christ, small groups should not be independent, but dependent on the church and its spiritual authority.

Small groups also pray. Prayer is absolutely essential to every aspect of the church's ministry. So all through the week Christians meet in various groups to pray for the work of the church, interceding for all the areas of congregational life discussed in this book: preaching, worship, fellowship, pastoral care, discipleship, evangelism, missions, and mercy. We should pray in our homes, with our families, at our Bible studies, and in all our meetings and classes. Every time we meet, we pray. And every time we pray, we throw more fuel onto the fire of the Spirit's ministry in the church.

As group members share their personal prayer requests, they start to care for one another, and also to minister to one another. They learn about practical needs within their group and within the wider body that they can help to meet. On occasion, as the situation requires, they offer one another spiritual counsel. As their relationships deepen, and as their love grows, they start to suffer and rejoice with one another. A small group is a place to share burdens and to get spiritual support for facing the hard situations of life. It is a place to listen and to be encouraged. It is a place for spiritual accountability and perhaps even for appropriate confession of sin. A healthy group can provide virtually all the spiritual care that someone needs, which is why it is good for every member of the body of Christ to belong to one.

Small groups can also be mobilized for ministry. The members may sponsor an investigative Bible study for friends who are unchurched, or they may work together to complete a service project in the church. To give just one simple example, a close-knit Bible study near Philadelphia gave a special Christmas gift to one of its members. She had just been diagnosed with an advanced form of cancer and was facing an uncertain future, as well as the painful prospect of a series of medical treatments. Upon learning that the woman's family would be in town for the holidays, the small group organized an elaborate feast. All the preparations were taken care of, so that on Christmas day the woman and her family could eat and drink, sing, and share special memories without distraction. Since the woman belonged to a small group within the larger body of Christ, she had loving Christian friends to care for her practical needs as well as to encourage her spiritual growth.

A PLACE TO BELONG

The kind of small groups we have been describing—in which a diverse group of Christians use their spiritual gifts to study the Bible, pray for God's work in the world, and care for one another, both spiritually and materially—promote the life and growth of the body of Christ. In these post-Christian times, many people are confused about their identity and are looking for a place to belong. The title character in Helen Fielding's novel *Bridget Jones* identifies herself as an "assured, receptive, responsive woman of substance." But then she seems to falter: "My sense of self comes not from other people but from . . . from . . . myself? That can't be right."[10]

And of course it's not right. We only discover our true identity when we join the body of Christ and begin to carry out the specific function God has assigned us. The place where we most belong is not our neighborhood, our nation, our company, or even our family, but our church—the city of God—that caring community where we are known and loved, and where we find deeply supportive faith-building relationships. This is why a Christian church for post-Christian times seeks to integrate every member of the congregation into Bible studies and other groups where individual needs can be met and each can minister to others.

5

Shepherding
God's Flock

✝

Pastoral Care

> "*My office, and that of every preacher and minister,
> does not consist in any sort of lordship but in serving all of you,
> so that you learn to know God, become baptized,
> have the true Word of God, and finally are saved.*"
>
> —◦ MARTIN LUTHER

When I was in the sixth grade my teacher confounded our class by reading a story out of sequence. Although I have forgotten the name of the book, it was a story about a boy who fought back against a bully. Several times a week she would read a chapter, chosen at random. As she skipped around the book, it was difficult (if not impossible) to follow the thread of the narrative. This reading method drew loud cries of protest from the class. Thoroughly exasperated, we tried to convince our teacher that this was no way to tell a story!

What our teacher was doing, although neither she nor we knew it at the time, was preparing us for life in postmodern times. The postmodern worldview can be defined in various ways, but one of its main features is the revolt against the "meta-narrative." A meta-narrative is a grand story that gives meaning to life. For Americans, the meta-narrative is a story about the triumph of democracy. For communists, it's about workers uniting to overthrow greedy capitalists. For evolutionists, it's about a natural process that produces intelligent life. But postmodernism says there are no meta-narratives, no overarching stories that give meaning to life. There are only the little stories that we make up as we go along. Human history is not one grand drama, but a vast collection of short autobiographies.

THE STORY OF ME

The revolt against the meta-narrative helps explain why people are so resistant to the gospel. Christianity has a story to tell. It claims to be *the* story, the story of humanity. It explains who we are, how we got here, and where we are going. We are creatures made in the image of God, who from all eternity has planned for us to give Him praise. Sadly, we have fallen into sin. But God entered human history to rescue us and redeem us through Jesus Christ, who died on the cross to pay for our sins and was raised from the dead to give us eternal life. Everyone who loves Jesus is destined to live with God forever. That's the story. *The* story. It's a story that hangs together, a story that makes sense of the world because it explains everything from before the beginning to "happily ever after." However, in these post-Christian times, people don't want to listen to God's story; they want to make up their own. When they read the script of salvation, they discover that it's all about God and His glory. But they were hoping to play a bigger part. Hence the postmodern revolt against the meta-narrative, which is really a rebellion against the authority of God.

The attack on the gospel story takes two basic forms. As we have seen, these post-Christian times are characterized by relativism and narcissism. The relativist attacks God's *intellectual* authority. He says, "I don't want anyone telling me what to believe; I demand the right to think what I want to think." The narcissist attacks God's *moral* authority. He says, "I don't want anyone telling me how to behave; I demand the right to do what I want to do." Relativism is a sin of the mind, a refusal to believe sound doctrine. Narcissism is a sin of the heart, a refusal to lead a holy life.

BOUGHT WITH HIS BLOOD

As surprising as it may seem, these are essentially the same issues that the apostle Paul faced in the first century. A good place to see this is Acts 20, the chapter that records Paul's farewell address to the Ephesian elders. The apostle was coming to the end of his ministry, so this speech marks the transition between the age of the apostles and the post-apostolic church, which continues to the present day.

It was a momentous occasion. Paul was hurrying to Jerusalem, and on his way he stopped at Miletus. There he sent for his dear friends, the elders of the church at Ephesus. Paul knew them well. He had planted their church himself. For three years he had labored with them in the gospel before continuing on his missionary journeys. Now the time had come to say good-bye. Paul said, "I know that none of you among whom I have gone about preaching the kingdom will ever see me again" (Acts 20:25). When he had finished his speech, "he knelt down with all of them and prayed. They all wept as they embraced him and kissed him. What grieved them most was his statement that they would never see his face again" (vv. 36–38a).

It was an emotional time for the Ephesians. They were saying farewell to their beloved pastor and friend. It was an emotional time for Paul, too, because he had an even heavier burden on his heart. In addition to his own sense of personal loss, he was concerned about the future of the church.

To appreciate his concern, it helps to remember how precious the church was. It was precious to Paul because he had planted it and then devoted three years of his life to help it grow, giving daily pastoral attention to the Ephesians. Even after he left them, he continued to have a shepherd's heart for their spiritual welfare. So the church was precious to Paul personally. But more important, it was precious to God, for Paul describes it as "the church of God, which he bought with his own blood" (Acts 20:28).

This verse has troubled some scholars because it speaks of the "blood of God." This is the only place where the Bible speaks this way. Of course God is spirit, and therefore, He does not have any blood. Obviously, then, this refers to the blood of Jesus Christ, the God-man, who bled and died on the cross for sinners. In fact, a better way to translate the verse is as follows: "the church of God, which he bought with the blood of his Own," meaning His own dear Son.

This shows why the church is so valuable. A purchase has been made—God shedding His own blood for our sins. To use the proper biblical term for it, we have been *redeemed*. "Redemption" is a word that comes from the marketplace. It is a commercial term used to describe salvation as a business transaction. The Bible often describes Christ's work on the cross in this way. We are "justified freely by his grace through the redemption that came by Christ Jesus" (Rom. 3:24), "who gave himself for us to redeem us from all wickedness" (Titus 2:14). Or again, God has rescued us from sin through "the Son he loves, in whom we have redemption, the forgiveness of sins" (Col. 1:13b–14).

Redemption always requires the payment of a ransom.[1] So the doctrine of redemption emphasizes the costliness of our salvation: "You were bought at a price" (1 Cor. 6:20). The price was the blood of the very Son of God, "for you know that it was not with perishable things such as silver or gold that you were redeemed from the empty way of life handed down to you from your forefathers, but with the precious blood of Christ, a lamb without blemish or defect" (I Pet. 1:18–19). Or as Paul once wrote to the Ephesians, "We have redemption through his blood, the forgiveness of sins" (Eph. 1:7). In salvation God has placed His valuation on the church. The price He has assigned is equivalent to the infinite merits of His Son, who shed His very own blood for our sins. As far as God is concerned, nothing in the whole world is more precious than the church of Jesus Christ.

ELDER, PASTOR, BISHOP

When we consider the high price of redemption, we can understand why Paul carried such a burden for the church: He wanted to protect God's investment! The apostle Paul perceived that the church was in grave danger, that as valuable as it was, it was also vulnerable. So he said to the Ephesian elders, "I know that after I leave, savage wolves will come in among you and will not spare the flock. Even from your own number men will arise and distort the truth in order to draw away disciples after them" (Acts 20:29–30). Of course, this is exactly what happened. Later Paul had to write to Timothy, who served as the church's pastor, with instructions to "command certain men not to teach false doctrines any longer" (I Tim. 1:3).

This shows that the church faced the same issues in the first century that we face in the twenty-first century. Not exactly the same, of course, because culture has changed. But sinners are sinners, and we always face the same temptation to make up our own story, and thus to defy God and His gospel. Furthermore, this temptation always comes in the same two areas: doctrine and life, or belief and behavior. The rebellion of the mind is to deny what God tells us to think (which today takes the form of relativism). The rebellion of the heart is to disobey what God commands us to do (which today takes the form of narcissism). Paul's fear was that after he was gone, the precious church of God would become morally and theologically corrupt.

What was the solution? How could the church preserve its doctrinal and ethical purity? Notice what Paul did *not* say. He did not tell the Ephesians to depend on the direct guidance of the Holy Spirit, because with the death of the apostles, they would no longer receive new revelation. Nor did Paul set up a one Christian/one vote democracy, in the hope that as long as they all read their Bibles, everything would work out fine. No, God's plan was to place the church under the care of shepherds.

In his farewell address in Acts 20, Paul uses three terms to describe these church leaders. The first term comes in verse 17, in which the apostle sends for the "elders of the church." The Greek word for elder is *presbuteros,* or "presbyter." Originally it came from the Jewish synagogue. In those days an elder was a man—often an older man—who held a position of spiritual authority among the people of God. But the term did not refer to age as much as to wisdom. An elder is a man who is mature in the faith.

The second term is "overseer," which comes from the word *episkopos,* often translated "bishop." In this case, *epi* means "over" and *skopos* means "look," so a bishop is someone who looks things over, who oversees. Whereas the term "elder" pertains to a leader's qualifications, this term refers to his function: A bishop is someone who has spiritual oversight in the church. He rules or governs.

The third term is "shepherd," or "pastor," from the Greek word *poimén.* Since the Bible has so much to say about shepherds, this term is especially rich in meaning. It is impossible to think of shepherds without thinking of David's prayer: "The LORD is my shepherd" (Ps. 23:1); or without singing Psalm 100: "We are his people, the sheep of his pasture"; or especially without remembering that Jesus is the Good Shepherd who looks for lost sheep (Luke 15:3–7) and even lays down His life for them (John 10:11). The reason the Bible so often calls us sheep is that we are totally dependent on God's care, the way sheep always are. And one of the primary ways He cares for us is by giving us shepherds after His own heart (Jer. 3:15)—pastors and elders who look after our souls.

What is striking about these three terms—elder, bishop, and shepherd (or pastor)—is that they are used interchangeably. All three titles are used to identify the same group of men. An elder is a bishop, and a bishop is a shepherd, or pastor. The same connection is made by the apostle Peter: "To the elders [presbuterous] among you . . . Be shepherds [poimanate] of God's flock that is under your care, serving as overseers [episkopountes]" (1 Peter 5:1–2; cf. Titus 1:5–7). This is a clue that the biblical pattern for spiritual leadership is not hierarchical, but collegial. God does not intend for bishops to rule the pastors, who in turn govern the elders. Instead, God has invested spiritual authority in a group of men—use whichever term for them you like—who together give wise counsel, spiritual oversight, and personal care to God's people. *A Christian church has a team of shepherds who provide loving pastoral care for every member of the church family.*

SHEPHERDS AFTER GOD'S OWN HEART

Good leadership is important, so it is necessary to know what the Bible teaches about shepherding. Who are the shepherds? How are they chosen? What do they do?

The first thing to know about the shepherds of God's flock is that they are chosen by God Himself. As Paul said to the elders from Ephesus, "Keep watch over yourselves and all the flock *of which the Holy Spirit has made you overseers"* (Acts 20:28a, italics added). No one ever decides to become a shepherd on his own. Only God can call a man into the ministry. The call comes partly through the inner work of the Holy Spirit, who convinces a man in his mind and heart that he is called to be an elder or a pastor. But the call also comes through the outward work of the Holy Spirit. If it is genuine, the shepherd's call will be recognized by others, and the church will ordain him with prayer and the laying on of hands.

In order to help churches identify the men God has called to serve as their spiritual leaders, the Bible provides the qualifications of a good shepherd. In a separate letter to Timothy, Paul gave the following list of minimum requirements:

> The overseer must be above reproach, the husband of but one wife, temperate, self-controlled, respectable, hospitable, able to teach, not given to drunkenness, not violent but gentle, not quarrelsome, not a lover of money. He must manage his own family well and see that his children obey him with proper respect. (If anyone does not know how to manage his own family, how can he take care of God's church?) He must not be a recent convert, or he may become conceited and fall under the same judgment as the devil. He must also have a good reputation with outsiders, so that he will not fall into disgrace and into the devil's trap. (1 Tim. 3:2–7; cf. Titus 1:5–9)

Incidentally, this and other Bible passages (especially 1 Tim. 2:11–15) make it clear that women are not called to serve as shepherds, but only certain men. The reason is that the church is God's household, and God's best plan for any house requires godly men to take spiritual responsibility for its welfare.

In his farewell address to the Ephesian elders, Paul did not take the time to rehearse all the qualifications for a shepherd.

Instead, he reduced them all to a single exhortation: "Keep watch over yourselves" (Acts 20:28). A shepherd is a man who takes spiritual care of his own soul, first of all. After all, how can he watch over anyone else, unless he knows how to watch over himself?

A good shepherd looks after his spiritual condition in two areas: heart and mind. Paul mentioned this to Timothy on another occasion. He wrote, "Watch your life and doctrine closely" (1 Tim. 4:16a). Both areas are equally important. For a shepherd to be doctrinally sound but morally loose would be scandalous. But no matter how godly he is, an elder or a pastor who is not orthodox in his theology eventually corrupts the purity of the church. So the Scripture implores the shepherds of God's flock to keep watch over themselves, both ethically and theologically.

This is difficult to do in post-Christian times. In an age of relativism, church leaders are pressured to compromise their theological views in order to avoid offending anyone, either inside or outside the church. And in an age of narcissism, pastors and elders are constantly encouraged to be selfish—to work for their own profit and to save time for their own interests. This makes Paul's exhortation as important for twenty-first-century shepherds as ever. Elders and pastors are called to master biblical theology, to spend time studying God's Word and learning the great doctrines of the Christian faith.

Every shepherd ought to aspire to be something of a Bible scholar and systematic theologian. Shepherds are also called to grow in godliness. This means leading a life of daily repentance, coming to a deeper conviction of sin so as to gain a firmer grasp of God's grace. It means leading a life of prayer, learning to commune with God and to intercede for the sheep of his flock. It means keeping in step with God's Spirit, growing in charity, humility, generosity, hospitality, and all the fruit of the Spirit. It means being devoted to his family, loving his wife, and training his children. This is all part of what it means to "keep watch over yourselves."

KEEPING WATCH

The reason it is so important for shepherds to watch their belief and their behavior is that they are called to oversee exactly the same things in the church. No sooner had Paul told the Ephesian elders to take care of their own spiritual lives than he proceeded to tell them to take spiritual care of everyone else: "Keep watch over yourselves *and all the flock*" (Acts 20:28, italics added).

A shepherd is a watchman. He watches that his sheep do not wander away. He watches to make sure that they get everything they need to eat and drink. He watches the weather in case they will need shelter. He watches for enemies to prevent any attack. Shepherding involves constant watchfulness. Otherwise, the sheep get lost or hurt.

The same is true in the flock of God, which is the church. Bishops, pastors, or elders have been given spiritual authority over every aspect of congregational life. Thus it is their responsibility to keep everything under their watchful care, including all the areas of church life that we have considered thus far in this book. They watch over the church's preaching, making sure that what is taught is true to God's Word. They watch over worship—including the music—making sure that it is according to Scripture. They watch over fellowship, making sure that every member of Christ's body is both giving and receiving spiritual care. And as we shall see in later chapters, shepherds also watch over discipleship, evangelism, missions, and mercy. They set the agenda and clarify the vision for every aspect of a church's ministry.

Shepherding God's flock is not a matter of running programs, however. A good shepherd gives personal attention to his sheep. Thus when pastors and elders are called to watch over the flock, they are called to take spiritual care of God's people. They are called to teach and visit them, encourage and exhort them, correct, counsel, and comfort them, and also to pray for them. They are called to help church members identify and exercise their spiritual gifts, to help resolve conflicts and settle disputes within the body, and to give spiritual advice for major life decisions. They are called to comfort the sick, the dying, and the bereaved. They are called to draw singles into close fellowship with God's family. They are called to help couples prepare for marriage, as well as to help them stay married afterward. They are also called to help parents raise their children in a godly way. In short, the shepherds of the flock are to serve God's sheep in every spiritual way they can.

Pastors and elders do not have to do all this work all by themselves. As we saw in the previous chapter, church members can give a good deal of spiritual care to one another, especially if they are involved in a Bible study or some other group in the church. Every Christian has a personal responsibility to nurture his or her spiritual life by staying connected to the body. However, in keeping with their God-given authority, spiritual shepherds have a responsibility to ensure that in one way or another, individual members of the flock are getting the care they need.

To help fulfill their calling, there are two practical things that pastors and elders in every church should do. One is to keep track of church membership in some formal way. Shepherds are required to know their sheep, and that includes knowing who belongs to the flock and who doesn't. The sheep who belong are those who profess to know Christ in a saving way, who are committed to living for His glory, who desire to be accountable to His body, who promise to support His church in its worship and work, and who thus submit to the spiritual authority of His shepherds.

There are indications throughout the New Testament that organized church membership was important to the first Christians. According to Luke, when people converted to Christianity they made a public commitment to Christ and were "added to their number" of believers (Acts 2:41, 47). Paul described Christians as "members of God's household" (Eph. 2:19), or as "those who belong to the family of believers" (Gal. 6:10). John distinguished between those who "belonged to us" and those who "did not really belong to us" (1 John 2:19). The elders of the early church knew who belonged to the body of Christ and who didn't. They kept track of who was in and who was out. This was essential to their work as shepherds. God held them accountable for the spiritual welfare of the sheep under their care (Heb. 13:17). How could they give an account to God without taking account of the members in their flock?

There are many ways for churches to keep track of their members. Obviously, it is useful for churches to have a central directory for their membership. The process for joining the church should include instruction about what it means to be a member and the opportunity to give a personal testimony to the church's pastors and elders. Many churches also find it helpful or even necessary to divide the congregation into groups for spiritual care, with each pastor or elder taking responsibility for a list of members. However it is done, every church should have its own shepherding plan—an organized strategy for providing spiritual care for every member.

The other practical thing that shepherds can and must do is to exercise church discipline. In its broadest sense, this neglected duty includes everything that pastors and elders do to promote the purity of the church. Preaching and teaching are forms of discipline because they help train people to be godly. Personal encouragement and private exhortation also help church members to live in a disciplined way. But more narrowly, church discipline refers to the correction of sin in the life of the church.

The proper way to handle church discipline is the way Jesus taught us to handle it in Matthew 18. The first step is to go to a church member privately. Hopefully, he will see the error of his ways and repent. But if private discipline proves to be ineffective, the next thing to do is to take along one or two other Christians to serve as witnesses. The third step is to inform the shepherds of God's flock, who should admonish him. At that point, if the offender still refuses to repent, he must be excommunicated, at least until such time as he turns away from his sin. For his own good and for God's glory, a person who claims to be a Christian yet refuses to live like one should be excluded from the fold (see 1 Cor. 5; Titus 3:10–11).

Although this process sounds simple, in practice it proves to be one of the most difficult aspects of pastoral ministry. It is essential to follow the biblical steps for discipline in the right order. Failure to follow the proper disciplinary procedures always causes a great deal of mischief, especially when people make matters public that God intends to be kept private. Dealing with sin is a messy business that requires both wisdom and courage from the shepherds of God's flock. And they can only exercise church discipline properly if they do it out of love for the holiness of God, zeal for the purity of the church, and compassion for the sinner himself.

Church discipline is a visible manifestation of God's moral authority, and thus it is part of the church's answer to narcissism. Many Americans have an antipathy to authority of any kind, but especially to moral authority. In his book *Moral Freedom*, sociologist Alan Wolfe contends that Americans still have a passionate concern for morality. However, they also insist on exercising moral autonomy, the right to determine their own ethical standards. "There is a moral majority in America," Wolfe writes. "It just wants to make up its own mind."[2]

The shepherds of God's flock stand against this kind of anti-authoritarianism by exercising moral authority in the church. This is necessary for the spiritual well-being of God's sheep. In these post-Christian times, Christians are as prone to be self-centered as anyone else. One of the ways that good shepherds help church members live for God and not for themselves is by holding them spiritually accountable. They preserve the identity of the church by distinguishing clearly between Christian and non-Christian conduct. When elders do not practice church discipline, people both inside and outside the church get confused about what it means to live like a Christian. Hence the need for those who keep watch to maintain good discipline.

WATCH OUT!

God's shepherds are called to keep watch over God's flock. But of all the things that need to be watched, the one that was of greatest concern to the apostle Paul was the church's theology. Indeed, this is one of his major concerns throughout his writings. Few things were more important to him than preserving sound doctrine.

The reason for this, of course, is that the early church was surrounded by false doctrine. The first Christians were constantly under theological attack. They were attacked by Jews who denied that Jesus was the Messiah. They were attacked by Romans who tried to make them worship the emperor. They were attacked by Greeks who promoted pagan philosophy. They were attacked by Gnostics who promised secret knowledge of spiritual truth. Then they were attacked by people who called themselves Christians but preached a different gospel, usually one based in some way on human effort rather than on divine grace.

The church faces a similar situation in the twenty-first century. In chapter 2 we identified four key areas where evangelical theology, under the influence of post-Christian ideas, is now under attack. There are new challenges to the authority of Scripture. There is a new openness to the idea that God is not absolutely sovereign. There is a new ambiguity about whether Jesus is the only way to God. And there is a new perspective on salvation that downplays the Reformation doctrine of justification by faith alone.

Where are these attacks coming from? In Paul's day they came from two different directions. One was from outside the church. Paul said, "I know that after I leave, savage wolves will come in among you and will not spare the flock" (Acts 20:29). But there was another source of theological error, one that must have sent a chill through the apostle's audience: "Even from your own number men will arise and distort the truth in order to draw away disciples after them" (Acts 20:30). The attack would come from *inside* as well as outside the church. This has proved to be the case, not only in Ephesus, but throughout the history of the church. Doctrinal error that leads a church astray almost never arises from the laity, but nearly always comes from the clergy. One of the most likely places for heresy to originate is from the church pulpit or the seminary lectern.

If that is true, then how can the church protect itself from theological error? It is up to the elders—the shepherds of God's flock—who are called to keep watch over the church in doctrine as well as in life. Proper oversight is essential to the moral and doctrinal health of the church. Good shepherds not only distinguish between Christian and non-Christian behavior, but they also discriminate Christian from non-Christian belief. This is why it is so important for pastors and elders to study theology. In order for a congregation to have any hope of preserving its doctrinal purity, its pastors and elders must be defenders of the faith.

Protecting and promoting sound doctrine is a matter of spiritual health. Theology is important, not simply for its own sake, but because its corruption inevitably causes spiritual damage in the lives of individual Christians. Consider the doctrinal challenges we mentioned above. Each of them has significant pastoral implications. Denying the authority of God's Word limits God's claim on our lives. Denying God's full sovereignty increases our anxiety about the future. Denying the uniqueness of salvation in Christ weakens our commitment to missions and evangelism. Denying that justification is by faith alone hinders our assurance of salvation. In each case, theology is connected to life. Ultimately it is for the sake of their sheep that the shepherds of God's flock keep careful watch over the church's doctrine.

A GOOD SHEPHERD

As the shepherds of Ephesus received their final instructions, they must have been daunted by the enormity of their task. If so, it would have helped them to remember that before he gave them this charge, the apostle Paul had set them a good example. His farewell address contained many reminders of the loving pastoral care he had given to their church.

Paul was a good shepherd. His ministry was bold. He never failed to do his duty, even when he was "severely tested by the plots of the Jews" (Acts 20:19), or when he faced prison and other hardships (Acts 20:23). The apostle's ministry was also evangelistic. This was how he summarized the content of his gospel message: "I have declared to both Jews and Greeks that they must turn to God in repentance and have faith in our Lord Jesus" (Acts 20:21). Paul never lost his focus on the basic message of salvation—repentance for sin and faith in Jesus Christ. And he communicated that message to everyone, constantly "testifying to the gospel of God's grace" (Acts 20:24).

Paul's ministry was biblical. He was always teaching the Bible. In fact, he was able to remind the elders that he had proclaimed to them "all the counsel of God" (Acts 20:27 KJV). At the same time, his ministry was practical. He not only taught the Bible, but he also applied it. He said, "You know that I have not hesitated to preach anything that would be helpful to you" (Acts 20:20a). In order to know what would be helpful to them, his ministry also had to be personal, and so it was. Paul exercised his ministry of God's Word in private as well as in public, for as he went on to say, "[I] have taught you publicly and from house to house" (Acts 20:20b). As we read Paul's letters, we find that he had extensive knowledge of the problems and personalities in each church he visited.

The apostle's ministry was costly. He led a life of self-sacrifice rather than self-preservation. Even his own life was "worth nothing" to him compared to the importance of fulfilling his calling as a shepherd of God's flock (Acts 20:24). Paul's ministry was passionate. Twice he mentioned the tears he shed for the Ephesians (Acts 20:19, 31). He had such great love for God's people in that church that he wept over their spiritual condition. His ministry was patient and persistent. He reminded the Ephesians, "For three years I never stopped warning each of you night and day with tears" (Acts 20:31). And finally, Paul's ministry was faithful to the very end. He declared, "I am innocent of the blood of all men" (Acts 20:26). In other words, he had fully discharged his responsibilities as a shepherd. He had done everything God called him to do for his flock. Paul summarized it all by saying, "In everything I did, I showed you that by this kind of hard work we must help the weak" (Acts 20:35).

Now that's a good shepherd! Paul performed the kind of shepherding that he could only have learned from Jesus Christ, the Chief Shepherd (1 Pet. 5:4). It is exactly the same kind of shepherding that the church needs in the twenty-first century. In order to become a teaching, worshiping, caring church that is growing by the power of the Holy Spirit, a congregation needs pastors and elders who reach the lost, teach God's Word, and serve God's people faithfully and passionately, even at great personal cost.

Who will answer this challenge? Where will such men be found? Who is willing to embrace the work of a spiritual shepherd as a long-term calling, a significant part of his life's work? Few men are both able and willing to serve as shepherds of God's flock. But consider what will happen if such men cannot be found. We live in a relativistic, narcissistic culture, in which people believe what they want to believe and behave the way they want to behave. And unless there are good shepherds to watch over God's flock, the same soul-destroying mind-set will corrupt the church, which is the most precious thing in the world.

The church's desperate need for faithful shepherds ought to move us to prayer, as it moved the apostle Paul. Near the end of his farewell address, he commended the Ephesian elders to God's care: "Now I commit you to God and to the word of his grace, which can build you up and give you an inheritance among all those who are sanctified" (Acts 20:32). Paul's prayers were answered. The Ephesian elders took their stand on God's Word, and as a result, they were built up in the faith and helped that church become a city on a hill. In the book of Revelation they are praised for defending their church from false doctrine. Then there is this commendation, to which every good shepherd aspires: "You have persevered and have endured hardships for my name, and have not grown weary" (Rev. 2:3).

6

Thinking and Acting Biblically

†

Discipleship

> *"In an age of relativity the practice of truth
> when it is costly is the only way to cause the world
> to take seriously our protestations concerning truth."*
>
> —◦ FRANCIS SCHAEFFER

Dietrich Bonhoeffer is famous for counting the cost of discipleship. Not only did the German theologian write a major book on the subject, but he also paid the price in his own Christian experience. Shortly before the end of World War II Bonhoeffer was executed for his opposition to Hitler. He became a living, dying example of his own maxim, that "when Christ calls a man, he bids him come and die."[1]

Bonhoeffer learned this principle from Jesus Christ, who often emphasized the difficulty of discipleship. As Jesus went around teaching His disciples, He was always saying things like, "If anyone would come after me, he must deny himself and take up his cross daily and follow me. For whoever wants to save his life will lose it, but whoever loses his life for me will save it" (Luke 9:23–24). Jesus never made it sound like following Him would be easy. On the contrary, He always told people that unless they were willing to give up everything, they could not be His disciples at all.

THE COST: EVERYTHING

From beginning to end, the Christian life is a life of sacrifice, of offering oneself to God for death. The Christian life not only begins that way, but it also continues that way. We are called to give our lives to God every day—dying to live. The apostle Paul wrote, "Therefore, I urge you, brothers, in view of God's mercy, to offer your bodies as living sacrifices, holy and pleasing to God—this is your spiritual act of worship" (Rom. 12:1). In this verse and the verse that follows, the apostle Paul counts the high cost of Christian discipleship. It comes at the price of a person's life.

The idea of offering a living sacrifice comes from the Old Testament, in which two kinds of sacrifices were prescribed: atonement and praise. A sacrifice of atonement was a blood offering to pay for sin. Obviously, that is not the kind of sacrifice Paul has in mind here, because Jesus has already made atonement for our sin by dying on the cross. "We have been made holy through the sacrifice of the body of Jesus Christ once for all" (Heb. 10:10). No further atonement is needed. There is nothing we can add to what Christ has done.

There was another kind of sacrifice, however, known as a thank offering. An animal was sacrificed, not to make atonement for sin, but simply to praise God for His mercy and grace. When Paul speaks of a "living sacrifice," this is the kind of sacrifice he has in mind: an offering of praise. This is confirmed by the end of the verse, which speaks of offering a living sacrifice as a "spiritual act of worship" (Rom. 12:1). The word Paul uses for worship—the Greek word *latreia*, which means "service"—is the biblical word for praising God in worship.

Paul's terminology is familiar to anyone who knows the Old Testament, but what he says is truly shocking. Instead of telling us to bring an offering, he urges us to *become* one. Ordinarily, when sacrifices were offered at the temple, a priest would take an animal and place it on the altar. In this case, however, we are told to climb on the altar and offer ourselves to God. We are not only the priests, but also the victims. If that seems morbid, remember that Paul is talking about *living* sacrifices. A dead offering would be of no use to God. But a living, breathing human being, who is "dead to sin but alive to God in Christ Jesus" (Rom. 6:11), is able to offer Him praise and worship. So God says, "Offer your bodies as living sacrifices" (Rom. 12:1).

When the Bible tells us to offer ourselves to God, it means our *whole* selves. Many Christians think of their Christianity as an important part of who they are, rather than everything they are. But God wants all of us. He doesn't want to make use of some of our talents; He wants us to dedicate them all to His glory. He doesn't want just a portion of our schedule; He wants us to serve Him all the time. He doesn't want us to give Him a piece of what we own; He wants us to recognize that it's all His stuff anyway. God even wants our bodies, so the Scripture tells us to offer our *bodies* as living sacrifices.

The mention of bodies comes as something of a surprise. Paul speaks this way partly because sacrifice traditionally involved the bodily death of an animal. However, many people view religion in spiritual terms rather than in physical terms. They think of their relationship to God as something inward and private, whereas Christianity actually teaches that a personal relationship with Jesus Christ transforms one's entire spiritual and physical existence. When we are told to become living sacrifices, therefore, it means that we should offer our whole selves to God, especially our bodies. Earlier Paul wrote, "Do not let sin reign in your mortal body so that you obey its evil desires. Do not offer the parts of your body to sin, as instruments of wickedness, but rather offer yourselves to God, as those who have been brought from death to life; and offer the parts of your body to him as instruments of righteousness" (Rom. 6:12–13). Our bodies do not belong to us, they belong to God, and therefore every part of us is to be used for His glory.

One man who understood what it means to offer one's whole self to God was the greatest American theologian, Jonathan Edwards. While he was still a young man, Edwards made the following notation in his journal:

> I have been before God, and have given myself, all that I am and have, to God; so that I am not, in any respect, my own. I can challenge no right in this understanding, this will, these affections, which are in me. Neither have I any right to this body, or any of its members—no right to this tongue, these hands, these feet; no right to these senses, these eyes, these ears, this smell, or this taste. I have given myself clear away, and have not retained any thing as my own. . . . I have been this morning to him, and told him, that I gave myself *wholly* to him. I have given every power to him. . . . I have this morning told him that I did take him for my whole portion and felicity, looking on nothing else as any part of my happiness . . . and that I would adhere to the faith and obedience of the gospel, however hazardous and difficult the confession and practice of it may be. . . . This, I have done; and I pray God, for the sake of Christ, to look upon it as a self-dedication, and to receive me now as entirely his own, and to deal with me, in all respects, as such, whether he afflicts me or prospers me, or whatever he pleases to do with me, who am his.[2]

Jonathan Edwards understood Christ's call to discipleship. If we intend to follow Christ, we must be give ourselves "clear away."

THE OBSTACLE: WORLDLINESS

Not many people are willing to offer themselves as living sacrifices. The price is too high! Discipleship demands everything we are and everything we have, which is more than most people are willing to pay, including many Christians.

Imagine what kind of influence the church would have on America if every Christian truly understood what it means to follow Christ. Imagine how it would change the political landscape, how it would affect the tone of public discourse and alter the legislative agenda. Imagine what a difference it would make for the urban poor, as entire communities were transformed by the power of Christian love. Imagine how it would affect media and the arts—everything from the priorities on the evening news to the paintings in the latest show. Imagine what effect costly Christian discipleship might have on public education, business ethics, or the legal system. Imagine what would happen to the average family. Or imagine what worship would be like. Imagine how many young people would commit themselves to a lifetime of Christian service. Or just imagine the conversations one would overhear on the bus or down at the local diner—free and open dialogues about spiritual things.

We can only imagine, because this is not what is happening. The reason for this is that most churchgoers assume that radical discipleship is only for advanced Christians, not for ordinary believers. It is this attitude that leads some people to think that they can receive Jesus as Savior without worshiping Him as Lord. It is nonsense, of course. The only Savior is the *Lord* Jesus Christ. But people do not want to submit to His lordship, so they imagine that it is possible to be *saved by* Christ without ever becoming a *servant of* Christ.

The result is that Christianity has less impact than it should. Two out of three Americans say that religion is gaining influence in their personal lives; however, 90 percent say that it is losing influence in America generally.[3] Combine the figures and the result is that Americans are getting more and more religious, but it is making less and less difference. The simplest explanation for this is that we do not understand Christ's call to discipleship. Hence the church's urgent need in these post-Christian times to provide Christian education that will inform, train, and disciple each member of the body of Christ. I say *education* because it is only by thinking biblically that we learn to act biblically, giving our whole selves to God.

It has never been easy to find people willing to pay the high price of Christian discipleship. It certainly wasn't easy in the time of Christ. When Jesus started adding up how much it would cost for someone to be one of His followers, "many of his disciples turned back and no longer followed him" (John 6:66). It wasn't easy in the time of Paul, either, which is why he had to warn the Romans not to "conform any longer to the pattern of this world" (Rom. 12:2a). This verse is often paraphrased: "Don't copy the behavior and customs of this world" (TLB); "Don't let the world around you squeeze you into its own mould" (J. B. Phillips); "Do not let the age in which you live force you into its scheme of thinking and behaving" (James M. Boice). The point is that what keeps most Christians from sacrificing everything for the cause of Christ is the pressure to think and act like non-Christians. It is hard to be a Christian in post-Christian times.

Another way to say all this is that the biggest obstacle to costly Christian discipleship is *worldliness.* The apostle James wrote, "Don't you know that friendship with the world is hatred toward God? Anyone who chooses to be a friend of the world becomes an enemy of God" (James 4:4). Thus we must choose between worldliness and godliness. In his book on the decline of the evangelical church, Iain Murray defined worldliness as "departing from God. It is a man-centred way of thinking; it proposes objectives which demand no radical breach with man's fallen nature; it judges the importance of things by the present and material results; it weighs success by numbers; it covets human esteem and wants no unpopularity; it knows no truth for which it is worth suffering."[4]

As we enter America's first post-Christian century, worldliness comes in all different shapes and sizes. There is scientific naturalism, the belief that matter is all that matters because the physical universe is the only ultimate reality. There is secular humanism, the perspective that because there is no God, human beings are at the center of their own universe. There is consumer materialism, for which the bottom line is always buying and selling. In one way or another, these worldly attitudes all stand in the way of dying to live for Jesus. As Douglas Webster asks, "How do we present Christ to a consumer-oriented, sex-crazed, self-preoccupied, success-focused, technologically sophisticated, light-hearted, entertainment-centered culture?"[5]

But perhaps the biggest barrier to costly discipleship is narcissism, the attitude that life is all about me. Earlier I referred to Christopher Lasch's classic work *The Culture of Narcissism*. In the book Lasch argues that in America selfishness has become part of the system. He did not conclude "that American society was 'sick' or that Americans were all candidates for a mental asylum but that normal people now displayed many of the same personality traits that appeared, in more extreme form, in pathological narcissism."[6] If Lasch is right, then the whole structure of post-Christian culture tends to produce extreme self-centeredness. The political process, the educational system, the news media, the entertainment industry—these cultural institutions constantly encourage the pursuit of personal gratification through power, money, sex, and pleasure.

In a culture of narcissism, what happens to the church? The answer is obvious: People only go to church if they can "get something out of it." Christianity is evaluated by the standard of self-interest; the church becomes just another product to consume. This probably explains why nearly 90 percent of evangelicals now believe that in salvation "God helps those who help themselves." The problem, of course, is that people who conform to the worldly pattern of narcissism will never willingly give themselves away for Jesus Christ or offer themselves up as living sacrifices. Even if they give themselves to God when they first come to Christ, they have trouble following the way of the cross thereafter. As has often been observed, living sacrifices have a way of crawling down from the altar.

David Wells, a keen observer of contemporary culture, explains what happens when people adapt Christianity to suit their own purposes. Such a religion, he writes,

> is quite different from the historical Christian faith. It is a smaller thing. . . . The self is a canvas too narrow, too cramped, to contain the largeness of Christian truth. . . . Good and evil are reduced to a sense of well-being or its absence, God's place in the world is reduced to the domain of private consciousness, his external acts of redemption are trimmed to fit the experience of personal salvation, his providence in the world diminishes to whatever is necessary to ensure one's having a good day. . . . Theology becomes therapy. . . . The biblical interest in righteousness is replaced by a search for happiness, holiness by wholeness, truth by feeling, ethics by feeling good about one's self. The world shrinks to the range of personal circumstances; the community of faith shrinks to a circle of personal friends. The past

recedes. The Church recedes. The world recedes. All that remains is the self . . . a paltry thing.[7]

The way to avoid such self-centered spirituality is to recognize that Christianity is not about what God can do for me, but about me giving my whole self to Him. This is why, in post-Christian times, Christianity is countercultural. To quote from Wells again, the Bible teaches that "the self is twisted, . . . maladjusted in its relationship to both God and others, . . . full of deceit and rationalizations, . . . lawless, . . . in rebellion, and indeed that one must die to self in order to live. It is this that is at the heart of the biblical gospel, this that is at the center of Christian character."[8] This is also what is at the heart of following Christ. Becoming a true disciple means rejecting the selfish pattern of this world in order to come and die for Christ.

THE MOTIVATION: GOD'S MERCY

What could possibly motivate someone to make that kind of personal sacrifice? It hardly seems to make sense. Why would people give themselves away, offering their very bodies as living sacrifices? Self-sacrifice goes against everything we have been taught to believe about self-interest.

If God expects people to make such a total sacrifice, then He must provide some extraordinary motivation for doing so. And this is exactly what He has done. The demand of Christian discipleship is made "in view of God's mercy" (Rom. 12:1a). The motivation for paying the high price of becoming a disciple is the most persuasive motivation that one can imagine: God's boundless mercy.

Mercy is the pity of God in not giving sinners what they deserve. What is significant about the way the word is used here in Romans 12:1 is that in the original Greek it occurs in the plural: "Therefore, I urge you, brothers, in view of God's *mercies*." The word "therefore" connects Romans 12 with everything else the apostle Paul has said in his letter to this point. In the first eleven chapters Paul laid out the whole plan of salvation, every stage of which is a manifestation of divine mercy. God shows His mercy in predestination, choosing sinners for salvation in Christ. He shows His mercy in justification, granting them the free gift of righteousness through the person and work of Jesus Christ. God shows His mercy in adoption, receiving lost sinners as His very own sons and daughters. He shows His mercy in sanctification, making His adoptive children holy like His one and only Son. God shows His mercy in perseverance, preserving His people through every struggle until they finally reach His glory. And He will show His mercy then, too, transforming every one of us into the glorious beauty of Christ.

As God carries out His plan of salvation, He shows mercy after mercy. It all comes through the cross, where Christ died for sinners. All of this—and more—is what the Bible means when it urges us to become living sacrifices "in view of God's mercy" (Rom. 12:1). We do not offer ourselves in order to get something from God, but in response to what He has already given. Christ died so that we might live; now we are dying to live for Him.

Once we get a clear view of God's mercy, it becomes evident that the only appropriate way to respond is by offering our whole selves for God's service. After urging us to offer our bodies as living sacrifices, Paul goes on to make this comment: "This is your spiritual act of worship" (Rom. 12:1b). The word "spiritual" is the Greek word *logikos*, which forms the basis for English words like "logical." It is perhaps best translated as "reasonable." So what's reasonable? What's reasonable is to take our whole lives—everything we are and have—place it on the altar, and give it up to God. That may sound unreasonable, but in view of God's mercy, it is actually the most reasonable thing we can do. God has shown His infinite mercy by offering His own Son for our sins. The only sensible way to respond is to offer ourselves in sacrifice for His service. In these post-Christian times, what enables us to overcome our desire to serve ourselves, and instead to pursue the path of costly discipleship, is the infinite mercy of God.

God's mercy is not just something God gave us in the past. It is also something He has for us in the present. At this very moment God's mercy is preserving us from destruction and leading us on to greater godliness. God has also promised to show us even more mercy in the future: "He who did not spare his own Son, but gave him up for us all—how will he not also, along with him, graciously give us all things?" (Rom. 8:32). Obviously Paul's question is rhetorical. Of course God will give us everything we need for salvation, from now until forever. Discipleship has its costs, but it also has its rewards—amazing, unimaginably vast rewards. Therefore, we serve God not simply out of a sense of obligation (although we are obliged to serve Him), but with a sense of anticipation. There will be mercy for us in the end, and also joy. "Let us fix our eyes on Jesus, the author and perfecter of our faith, who for the joy set before him endured the cross, scorning its shame, and sat down at the right hand of the throne of God. Consider him who endured such opposition from sinful men, so that you will not grow weary and lose heart" (Heb. 12:2–3).

THE METHOD: MIND RENEWAL

What is God's method of discipleship? How do we become better disciples? Discipleship starts with the mind. The offering of our bodies as living sacrifices, in response to God's mercy, comes through the renewing of our minds: "Do not conform any longer to the pattern of this world, but be transformed by the renewing of your mind" (Rom. 12:2a). This is God's basic method for discipleship—what James Montgomery Boice called *Mind Renewal in a Mindless Age.*[9]

In Romans 12:2 there is an obvious contrast between "conform" and "be transformed." Both words have to do with formation—with what a person is becoming. In the original Greek both are also passive verbs. That is to say, they do not describe something a person does, but something done *to* a person. The difference between the two words is who does the forming. In the case of "conform," it is the world that does the forming: "Do not conform [literally, be conformed] . . . to the pattern of this world" (Rom. 12:2). Given the opportunity, the world always tries to adapt us to its way of thinking and acting. We don't even need to try to conform to the world; it just happens. When it comes to the verb "transform," however, the one who does the forming is God. He does not tell us to transform ourselves, but to *be* transformed. The transformation comes through the supernatural work of His Holy Spirit. Discipleship is not a self-help program for improving personal spiritual performance; the transforming change comes from God.

Another difference between being conformed and being transformed is how and where the change takes place. Conforming usually works from the outside in. Wrong actions promote wrong ideas. Conformation starts with keeping up appearances, with trying to live the way the world lives, but soon the conformist also starts to think the way the world thinks. To put this into the categories we have been using to describe these post-Christian times, the narcissist becomes a relativist. By contrast, being transformed works from the inside out. God's Spirit begins His life-changing work at the very center of a person's being. To use the Greek term for it, the disciple undergoes a "metamorphosis." A radical transformation takes place in which the Christian is turned spiritually inside out.

The disciple's transformation starts with the development of a thoroughly Christian mind. As the Scripture says, "Do not conform any longer to the pattern of this world, but be transformed *by the renewing of your mind*" (Rom. 12:2a, italics added). Mind renewal is the work of God's Holy Spirit, who accomplishes this transforming work as we read, study, and meditate on God's holy Word.

We are living in a mindless age, in which people are unwilling and unable to think reflectively about very much of anything, let alone how to really live. Sociologists call this "the dumbing down of America." The process of intellectual atrophy is accelerated by the trivializing effect of television, which damages the life of the mind by exalting the image over the word. This is the age of the sound byte and the remote control, which keep us from thinking about anything for more than a few seconds.

What we ought to do is take the time to stop and think. That is what people usually do when they lose their way. A motorist looking for a street in a strange neighborhood eases off the gas pedal and turns down the stereo. But in these post-Christian times, we do exactly the opposite. We sense that we have lost our spiritual way, but instead of taking time to think things through, we go faster and faster, cranking the music louder and louder.

Disciples are called to be different. God's method for training us to follow Christ starts with the renewing of our minds. This is not merely an intellectual exercise. Ideas always have consequences. God transforms our minds with the specific intention of changing our whole lives. First, our thoughts influence our affections, for in time we come to feel what we believe. Then we start to say what we think and do what we think. So the important thing is to get our thinking straight. Then we will know how God wants us to feel and what He wants us to say and to do. Ultimately, it is by thinking biblically that we learn how to live biblically. *Therefore, a Christian church for post-Christian times provides an effective Christian education program to inform, train, and disciple all members of the congregation.*

An effective Christian education program provides *information* —biblical information for a Christian view of the world. This starts with a biblical view of God, the study of His divine attributes. It continues with a biblical view of humanity in sin and salvation, and with a biblical view of God's plan for human history: creation, fall, grace, and glory. This information needs to be biblical in order to combat the prevailing relativism of our age. God has provided the answer to relativism in His revelation. An effective Christian education program also provides *training*. It offers practical instruction for how to study the Bible, worship God, live as a spiritual family, share the gospel, support world missions, and serve others with deeds of mercy.

This kind of informing, training, discipling education is necessary at every stage of the Christian life. It is necessary for children. When children are taught how to think and act biblically, they can offer God a whole lifetime of useful service. Christian education is equally necessary for young adults who are making life choices that will chart their future and who want to know God's will. It is necessary for parents hoping to raise their children in a godly way, and also for singles looking to find their place in the church and the world. Discipleship is for Christians of all ages because the transformation never stops. Some of the most exciting people in the world are older Christians who are still hungry to learn as much about God as they can. Mind renewal is a continuous process that lasts to the very end of the Christian life.

Churches can set up all kinds of programs to teach people how to love God with all their minds. The most important thing is preaching, the exposition of God's Word. In chapter 4 we also emphasized the importance of studying the Bible in smaller groups. Every church should have some kind of Bible school program, not only for children, but also for adults. This should include instruction in Bible, theology, church history, and practical Christian living. Children especially should be trained in catechism and Bible memory. When possible and where needed, churches should start their own schools. They should set up libraries and bookstores to introduce people to great Christian literature. Where possible, they should also use radio and the Internet to disseminate biblical teaching. There are many effective ways to teach and train for the renewal of the mind.

Yet a church could run all these programs and still fail in the area of discipleship. God's method is mind renewal. However, His goal is not simply the discipleship of the mind, but the transformation of the whole Christian. Some churchgoers expand their minds without ever undergoing the total transformation that God intends for every disciple. The point of mind renewal is to offer God not only the mind, but the whole self for His service. After all, a mind cannot climb up on the altar all by itself. When a Christian mind is truly offered as a sacrifice of praise to God, then Christian eyes, arms, feet, and everything else will be offered as well.

All of this leads to a practical question for every Christian to answer: Am I living a life of radical Christian discipleship? Here are some more questions: Am I finding deeper satisfaction with God in worship? Do I have a growing hunger to pray and to study God's Word? Is my heart growing more tender toward others, especially people I find it hard to love? Am I serving my family and friends in ways that can lead them closer to Christ? Do I have an increasing desire and ability to glorify God in my daily work? Am I standing for Christ in my community? Do I have a growing and tangible commitment to world missions? Am I actively pursuing friendships with people who need to hear the gospel? Am I becoming more patient with life's difficulties and disappointments, both large and small? Am I using my money in sacrificial ways that reflect my ultimate spiritual priorities? Am I exercising better judgment about my use of free time? Am I reaching out to anyone in mercy, seeking nothing in return? Am I maintaining total sexual purity? Am I thinking less of myself and more of others? And most important of all, am I really growing in my love for Christ?

These are only a few of the ways that we are called to think and to act biblically. Jesus said that His disciples need to be taught how to obey *everything* He has commanded (Matt. 28:20a). Yet the questions in the previous paragraph are a good place to start. If we are not growing in these areas, then the Bible urges us to offer ourselves as living sacrifices, holy and pleasing to God. After all, in view of God's many mercies, this is only reasonable. And then the Bible urges us not to be conformed any longer to the pattern of these post-Christian times, but to be transformed by God's renewing of our minds.

7

Reaching the World

†

Missions and Evangelism

> "*Missions is not the ultimate goal of the church. Worship is.
> Missions exists because worship doesn't. Worship is ultimate,
> not missions, because God is ultimate, not man. . . . Worship,
> therefore, is the fuel and goal in missions. It's the goal of
> missions because in missions we simply aim to bring the nations
> into the white-hot enjoyment of God's glory. The goal of
> missions is the gladness of the peoples in the greatness of God."*
> —JOHN PIPER

It is hard to find Christians who are willing to pay full price for discipleship. In these self-absorbed, truth-resistant times, many people make decisions for Christ without ever intending to offer their entire lives for His service. This unwillingness to make sacrifices is harmful to the church in many ways, but it is especially injurious to the cause of world missions. Missionary recruiters find it increasingly difficult to identify people who are willing to devote themselves to a lifetime of Christian ministry, especially if it promises to be difficult or dangerous. Despite the popularity of short-term mission trips, the number of career missionaries is down, and some experts fear a critical shortage in the coming decades. This is a sign that something is seriously wrong. A genuine passion for God's glory inevitably leads to a firm commitment to reach the lost—those who do not have a personal saving relationship with Jesus Christ, without which they will be condemned to spend eternity in hell. Where this compassionate commitment is lacking, there must be a general lack of spiritual vitality.

Various attempts have been made to explain the decline of missions in America, but the basic issue is discipleship. A failure to count the cost of following Christ inevitably hinders one's commitment to the global work of His gospel. The vital connection between missions and discipleship is explained by two veteran missionary doctors—Tom and Cynthia Hale—in a passionate letter entitled "Disciples Needed for the Twenty-First Century." The Hales write:

> Our major concern relates to the level of discipleship we have observed during our travels: we fear it is too shallow. . . . During the past generation, the worldwide evangelical church has experienced unprecedented growth; in terms of the plain numbers coming to Christ, nothing like it has been seen before. But in the midst of this good news, there are troubling signs that many of these new believers are continuing to follow Christ primarily for what they can receive, rather than for what they can give. . . .
>
> We have . . . a lingering sense that some . . . rapidly growing churches are placing more emphasis on drawing people in than on sending people out. They have been placing more emphasis on the blessings of following Christ than on the cost. The "hard" teachings are downplayed; it's as if there is a fear of scaring people away. . . .
>
> The main work of the church is to prepare those who are being drawn in to then be thrust out into the world as witnesses. . . . The question is often asked: "How can we recruit more long-term missionaries?" The answer, we believe, is for churches to place greater emphasis on discipling their members, on challeng-

ing their members to deny self, to forsake all, and to follow Christ with no conditions or limitations—in other words, to "sell out" to Christ.[1]

If this analysis is correct, as I believe it is, then the future of missions depends on the church's recovery of the kind of radical Christian discipleship we discussed in the previous chapter.

A DANGEROUS MISSION

But what's so important about missionary work, anyway? *Is it still important?* What does "missions" mean today? And does it matter whether the American church continues to play a leading role in global evangelism?

Missionary work matters because it is central to God's plan to glorify Himself all over His world. One of the last gifts Jesus gave to the church was a clear, unambiguous statement of its mission to the world. Jesus said, "All authority in heaven and on earth has been given to me. Therefore go and make disciples of all nations, baptizing them in the name of the Father and of the Son and of the Holy Spirit, and teaching them to obey everything I have commanded you" (Matt. 28:18–20a).

That Great Commission is still in effect. Although it was first given to the apostles, it is a mission statement for all Christians at all times and in all places. The first Christians—not just the apostles, but also ordinary church members—"preached the word wherever they went" (Acts 8:4). We too are on a mission to make disciples who will offer themselves to God for His service. We do this by going to all nations, baptizing them in God's triune name, and then teaching them to obey all the commands of Christ. The question is, How should we carry out that mission in the twenty-first century? What is the situation in the world today, and how is the church called to respond?

One way to answer these questions is to study what Jesus said about world evangelism and the end of history. In Matthew 24 Jesus warned His disciples about the destruction of the temple in Jerusalem. Naturally, they were curious to know when this would take place, so they asked Jesus, "When will this happen, and what will be the sign of your coming and of the end of the age?" (Matt. 24:3b). The disciples assumed that these events (the destruction of the temple and the end of history) would take place at the same time. They didn't realize that they were really asking two separate questions. Thus they probably didn't understand the answer, either, because Jesus answered both questions at once. In addition to describing what would soon happen to the temple, and to the apostles themselves, He made a prophecy about the church's destiny.

This broad perspective is especially evident in Matthew 24:9–14. This passage contains vital teaching about the future of the church's mission to the world. First, the mission will be dangerous. Jesus said, "Then you will be handed over to be persecuted and put to death, and you will be hated by all nations because of me. At that time many will turn away from the faith and will betray and hate each other, and many false prophets will appear and deceive many people. Because of the increase of wickedness, the love of most will grow cold" (Matt. 24:9–12). The apostles faced all of these physical and spiritual hardships. The historical records show that they were hated, persecuted, and martyred. Their personal correspondence reveals how they confronted apostasy, false doctrine, immorality, and lovelessness in the early church.

Yet these are the same difficulties that the church has faced in every age, and never more so than in the twentieth century. Verse 9 describes the persecution Christians face from enemies outside the church: torture and martyrdom for the sake of Christ. This has been happening all over the world. Think of the systematic deportation of Christians to the Soviet gulags, or the repression of the underground church in China, or the Christians killed in Muslim lands. The twentieth century will go down as the bloodiest in human history. More Christians were killed for their faith in the twentieth century than in the first nineteen centuries of church history combined, and according to some estimates, many thousands more are martyred every year.[2] Although this is shocking, it is not surprising. Jesus said, "You will be handed over to be persecuted and put to death, and you will be hated by all nations because of me" (Matt. 24:9). Jesus knew that His followers would be hated and killed precisely because they were His followers.

At the same time that the church suffers hatred from the outside world, it also faces hardship from within its own ranks. Verse 10 is about apostasy, about professing Christians falling away from the faith: "At that time many will turn away from the faith and will betray and hate each other." Verse 11 goes on to speak of heresy, of church leaders perverting the true doctrine of salvation: "And many false prophets will appear and deceive many people" (Matt. 24:11). Then verse 12 is about apathy, about genuine believers losing their love for one another and for God. Jesus said, "Because of the increase of wickedness, the love of most will grow cold" (Matt. 24:12). Today all these things are happening all over the world. We seem to be facing what Jesus called an "increase of wickedness" (Matt. 24:12). And wherever there is persecution, some church members deny Christ in an effort to escape, while many others lose their boldness for proclaiming the gospel.

The church's suffering seems to be getting more intense. Although it is sometimes difficult to distinguish between the victims of politically or ethnically motivated violence and the true martyrs of the faith, hundreds of thousands of Christians were killed during the twentieth century. It is too early to tell what the twenty-first century will bring, but it is certain that the persecution will continue. This is a time of tribulation, and we should not expect to escape. God's plan for evangelizing the world calls for Christians to suffer and die as they share the love of Christ. There is an incarnational aspect to our mission that requires us to participate in the sufferings of Christ (see Phil. 3:10–11). Hence the absolute necessity of counting the cost of discipleship, especially when we are surrounded by narcissism. It is dangerous to be a Christian, and unless we are willing to offer ourselves as living sacrifices, we will never be able to carry out God's mission to the world. So, in order to give us the courage to live and die for our faith, Jesus has given us this promise: "He who stands firm to the end will be saved" (Matt. 24:13).

A MISSION WITH A MESSAGE

Before embarking on a dangerous mission, it is important to know exactly what the mission requires. In this case, the church has been given a mission with a message. Jesus said, "This gospel of the kingdom will be preached in the whole world" (Matt. 24:14a).

The word "gospel" means "good news." Where there is good news, usually there is also bad news, so what's the bad news? The bad news is that we are guilty of sinning against a holy God, and therefore we are under His condemnation. The Bible teaches that "all have sinned and fall short of the glory of God" (Rom. 3:23). It teaches further that "the wages of sin is death" (Rom. 6:23a), meaning spiritual death in the present life and eternal separation from God and His glory in the life to come (2 Thess. 1:9–10). Here is more bad news: There is nothing we can do to escape God's judgment. There is no good deed we can perform, no penance we can endure, no pilgrimage we can complete that will make us right with God.

There is good news, however. Jesus called it the "gospel of the kingdom" (Matt. 24:14). He had been preaching it from the outset of His public ministry. Near the beginning of His gospel, Matthew told how "Jesus went throughout Galilee, teaching in their synagogues, preaching the good news of the kingdom, and healing every disease and sickness among the people" (Matt. 4:23). God's kingdom is simply God's rule. It is His royal authority, which He exercises through Jesus, His chosen King. Therefore, when Jesus told people the good news of the kingdom, He was announcing that He had come to reign as King.

Jesus entrusted this royal message to His church. Our mission is to take the good news of the kingdom and to spread it all over the world. Once Jesus died and rose again, the good news got even better. The good news of the gospel is salvation from sin through the crucifixion and resurrection of Jesus Christ (see 1 Cor. 15:4). Jesus died on the cross to pay the penalty for sin. Once He was raised from the dead, the free gift of eternal life was His to give away. Now everyone who believes in Jesus receives the forgiveness of sins. Through faith in Christ, we are no longer under condemnation; God's blessings belong to us forever. This is the gospel we proclaim. Our mission is to tell the whole world about salvation through the crucified and risen Christ.

Sadly, that message is now under attack. We have already seen how the doctrines of God, Scripture, and salvation are being assaulted, even in the evangelical church. But the crucial issue for missions is the uniqueness of Jesus Christ. Is Jesus the only way to God?

In these post-Christian times, many people say that there are many ways to God. They claim that the major world religions are all equally true. Each provides a piece of the truth, a valid interpretation of the way things are and ought to be. Even religion has become relative: If Christianity is true at all, it is only relatively true.

What is most alarming is that religious relativism is starting to come to church. Some so-called evangelicals claim that it is possible for people to be saved without having personal faith in Jesus Christ. Christians have always been concerned about what will happen to people who have never heard the gospel. This concern used to compel Christians to become foreign missionaries; now it seems to make them rethink their theology. In a book called *A Wideness in God's Mercy: The Finality of Jesus Christ in a World of Religions*, Clark Pinnock argues that non-Christian religions offer true but partial salvation. Somehow the saving work of Jesus Christ is revealed through other religions. Jesus can save people through Buddhism or Islam as well as through Christianity.

This is not the place to list all the reasons that this kind of religious relativism is biblically and theologically indefensible. However, it *is* the place to consider its alarming implications for world missions. Obviously, it makes a tremendous difference whether Muslims can be saved by being good Muslims, or whether they need to come to explicit faith in Jesus Christ. Certainly missionary work would be a good deal easier if people could become Christians without changing religions! This is why some missionaries are tempted to rearrange and reinterpret Christianity to fit the local religious context. Christian contact with other religions sometimes leads to syncretism, in which the gospel is conformed to meet pagan expectations. But Christ does not conform; He confronts. While the gospel must be translated in a way that people in every culture can understand, the good news itself never changes. It is always salvation in Christ *alone*. He is the one and only way to get right with God.

If Jesus saves people through other religions, then why did He commission us to preach the gospel to the whole world, especially when that mission is so dangerous? What is the point of sacrificing everything to tell others about Jesus if trusting Him as the unique Savior of the world is not even necessary for salvation? The truth is that personal faith in Jesus Christ is essential to salvation. Peter said, "Salvation is found in no one else, for there is no other name under heaven given to men by which we must be saved" (Acts 4:12). The phrases that refer to the Savior are exclusive ("no one else," "no other name"), while the phrases that refer the people He saves are inclusive ("under heaven," "given to men"). God has given only one Savior, and He is for everyone.

Paul spoke in similar terms when he said, "Everyone who calls on the name of the Lord will be saved." Then he asked, "How, then, can they call on the one they have not believed in? And how can they believe in the one of whom they have not heard? And how can they hear without someone preaching to them?" (Rom. 10:13–15). The answer, of course, is that the nations cannot be saved unless they hear and believe the gospel of the cross and the empty tomb. We are on a mission with a message, a mission based on the fact that people simply cannot be saved unless they know Jesus.

A GLOBAL MISSION

If Jesus is the world's only Savior, then obviously the whole world needs to know about Him. So the church has been given a global mission. Each of the mission statements in the New Testament emphasizes the global reach of the gospel: "Go and make disciples of all nations" (Matt. 28:19); "As you sent me into the world, I have sent them into the world" (John 17:18); "And this gospel of the kingdom will be preached in the whole world as a testimony to all nations" (Matt. 24:14).

It is significant that the gospel is preached as a *testimony* to the nations. We are commissioned to tell people the good news about the cross and the empty tomb as clearly and as plainly as we can. It is for them to accept or reject. Sometimes our testimony is accepted; other times it is rejected. Our job is simply to testify to the salvation that God has provided in Jesus Christ. The results are up to God. To evangelize is not to make converts (which is something only the Holy Spirit can do, anyway), but to present the gospel, regardless of what happens as a result.

In Matthew 24:14 Jesus uses two different phrases to show that the church's mission is global. One phrase is geographic; the other is ethnic. "In the whole world"—this refers to world geography. God intends the good news about Jesus Christ to be preached everywhere in the whole world. The gospel will go to each and every territory. The other phrase is "to all nations." Today the word "nation" usually refers to a political state. However, in biblical Greek the word is *ethné*, which forms the basis for English words like "ethnic" and "ethnicity." It does not refer to countries, but to cultural communities. In biblical terms, nations are ethnic groups that share a common cultural identity. Missiologists call them "people groups." Definitions vary, but according to the 1982 Lausanne Strategy Working Group, a people group is "a significantly large grouping of individuals who perceive themselves to have a common affinity for one another because of their shared language, religion, ethnicity, residence, occupation, class or caste, situation, etc. or combinations of these."[3]

When Jesus promised that the gospel would be preached to all nations, He meant that it would reach every *people group*. Many Bible verses make this promise.[4] Therefore, our commission is to proclaim the good news, not only in all places, but also to all peoples. When God announced His covenant with Abraham, He said, "All peoples on earth will be blessed through you" (Gen. 12:3b). God instructed His people to "declare his glory among the nations, his marvelous deeds among all peoples" (Ps.

96:3). He said, "I . . . am about to come and gather all nations and tongues, and they will come and see my glory" (Isa. 66:18). God has always planned that "repentance and forgiveness of sins will be preached in [Jesus'] name to all nations" (Luke 24:47). This promise is being fulfilled in the twenty-first century as many churches and mission agencies place a special emphasis on getting the gospel to people who have never been reached.

The reason the gospel must be preached to all nations is that God demands the praise of all nations. He says, "I am God; I will be exalted among the nations" (Ps. 46:10). In response, His people say, "All the nations you have made will come and worship before you, O LORD; they will bring glory to your name" (Ps. 86:9). These promises are confirmed in the book of Revelation. There, in his vision of glory, the apostle John saw "a great multitude that no one could count, from every nation, tribe, people and language" (Rev. 7:9a; cf. 5:9), standing before God and giving Him all their praise. God is calling the nations to worship, seeking to glorify Himself in the praise of all peoples.

Universal praise is the ultimate purpose of missions and evangelism. Our mission to the world is for the greater glory of God. The church has had this global vision since the very beginning. Jesus told His apostles, "You will be my witnesses in Jerusalem, and in all Judea and Samaria, and to the ends of the earth" (Acts 1:8b). This is exactly what happened. It started with the first church of Jerusalem, a small group of Christians who started reaching the world for Christ. For the last two thousand years, Christians have been preaching the gospel to new people in new places at every opportunity. Christians are still doing it today, with the result that more and more people are giving praise to God all the time. The whole church has been taking the whole gospel to the whole world, so that all nations may give all the glory to God.

MISSION ACCOMPLISHED?

Jesus promised that once we preach the gospel to all people, in all places, our mission will be accomplished: "This gospel of the kingdom will be preached in the whole world as a testimony to all nations, *and then the end will come*" (Matt. 24:14, italics added). What Jesus meant by "the end" was the end of history. Jesus has promised to come back to the earth in power and glory, but not until we complete His mission to the world.

Although Jesus did not state how much time would elapse between the preaching of the gospel and the coming of the end, He gave the impression that the latter would immediately follow the former. Other Bible passages suggest the same thing. There is the Great Commission, which Jesus ended with the promise to be with us to the end of the present age (Matt. 28:20b). There are the words of Peter, who exhorted Christians not simply to wait for God's great day, but actually to hasten its arrival (2 Pet. 3:12). The implication is that in some way the work of missions serves to speed the coming of Christ. Then there is the promise from Revelation, in which the martyrs in heaven are told to wait "a little longer, until the number of their fellow servants and brothers who were to be killed as they had been was completed" (Rev. 6:11). So the Bible gives several clues about what must happen before the end will come. And one key factor that determines when the world will end is the church's fulfillment of its missionary mandate.

The fact that the gospel must be preached everywhere to everyone gives real urgency to the task of world missions. However, this fact has also misled Christians into trying to predict the timing of the Second Coming. Mission agencies speak of "the unfinished task," and then try to set a timetable for finishing it. This happened back in 1910, when the famous Edinburgh Conference on world missions proposed "world evangelization in this generation." More recently, a movement called "AD2000 and Beyond" wanted "a church for every people and the gospel for every person by A.D. 2000." Obviously, those targets were never reached. Now the date has been moved back twenty-five years, with new goals set for Bible translation, church planting, and unreached people groups by 2025. This led one speaker at Amsterdam 2000, another landmark global conference on world missions, to conclude: "At the second millennial turn, while no one can know the precise conclusion of history, we are now certain that we are within range of finishing the task, with more momentum than ever before. For the first time in history it is possible to see the end of the tunnel, when there will be a church movement within the language and social structure of every people group on earth, powerful face-to-face evangelism taking over within all peoples."

It is good to be ambitious for the gospel, to have a real sense of urgency about evangelism, and perhaps even to set specific targets for world missions. Christ is coming soon—the sooner, the better!—and our work helps to prepare for His coming. However, there is a danger in turning the global work of the gospel into a human enterprise, a job that human beings are capable of completing in order to compel the return of Christ. Some missionary leaders seem to assume that we have a finite task that we are close to finishing; yet in reality, there is still a vast amount of work to be done. Consider the following statistics:

- One-third of the people in the world today claim to be Christians of one kind or another; however, according to the best estimates, no more than one in ten has genuine faith in Jesus Christ.
- Perhaps three billion people or more have never heard the gospel presented in any form. Estimates vary, but by any measure, the world contains at least 10,000 unreached

people groups—cultural communities in which there is no significant Christian presence.

- Some 250 ethnic groups with populations of 10,000 or more do not have any Christian workers planned for them. Not only are they unreached, but there are no plans to reach them. Also, some five hundred people groups are without a church planter.
- Of the more than 6,500 different languages in the world today, more than four thousand do not have any portion of the Bible available.

But beyond these statistics, consider the mission itself, which is to *disciple* the nations (Matt. 28:19). This means much more than simply preaching an evangelistic sermon and then going back home. Missiologist Andrew Walls explains, "Discipling a nation involves Christ's entry into the nation's thought, the patterns of relationship within that nation, the way the society hangs together, the way decisions are made.... National discipleship involves a generational penetration of the ways of thought, the springs of action, the points of reference, of people forming a nation."[5] By that definition, even nations that have the gospel still need to be discipled (like the United States of America, to name one). Bringing the peoples of the world under the lordship of Christ will take many years of patient discipleship.

It is not at all certain, therefore, that the unfinished task will or even can be completed during the present generation. Its completion is unlikely to fit our own projections, but of course we do not tell God when it is finished. Our global mission will be accomplished when God tells us it is accomplished, which He will do by sending His Son back in triumph at the end of days. Of course Christ can come at any time; the timing is up to God. Yet it seems as though the unfinished task will not be finished in our lifetime. The point of saying this is not to dampen our zeal for global evangelism, but rather to emphasize that this task requires a long-term commitment. The end might or might not come in the next hundred years. Either way, our task remains the same, and there is always more work to be done. We are called to keep spreading the gospel until Jesus comes again. *Thus a Christian church for post-Christian times advances the missionary work of Christ in the local community and throughout the world.*

OUR MISSION

How can we advance this work? What can we do to help meet the goal of missions, which is the glory of God? In the twenty-first century, what specific role has God given the American church in accomplishing His mission to the world?

There is no longer any clear consensus about how to do missionary work. In recent decades experts have found it hard to agree on the most effective strategies for supporting indigenous churches, communicating across cultures, using information technologies, evangelizing Muslims, or meeting other major mission goals. Missions seems to be getting more complicated, which makes it hard for churches to establish clear missionary priorities. However, there are at least three commitments that every congregation should make.

The first is to *support the church in other parts of the world.* Most American churches have resources to share with other Christians. Some of these resources are spiritual. In areas like theological training, for example, we have spiritual gifts to share with the church around the world. We can also pray for the church's worldwide work, especially in places where Christians face hardship and persecution. Other resources are financial. When it is used wisely, American money can help publish Christian literature, broadcast biblical teaching, build churches and seminaries, and provide disaster relief in the name of Christ.

What kind of work should we support? We should support indigenous churches, first of all. Without fostering dependence on American aid, we can help the pastors and teachers who are best equipped to reach their people with the gospel.[6] Only a local church is able to do the complete work of evangelism and discipleship, so we should support local efforts around the globe. Rather than seeking to gain control, we should give money and ministry in ways that help others reach their cultures for Christ. We should place a special priority on city work. The world is facing an urban future. In recent decades more than a billion people have moved from the country to the city. It is estimated that by the end of the twenty-first century more than 80 percent of the world's population will live in cities. This gives the city strategic importance in world missions, not only now, but for the foreseeable future. We should support youth work. There are more than two billion people in the world under fifteen years of age. Imagine the world-wide impact of reaching them for Christ.

Then there are the unreached peoples, which should also be a focus of American concern. This brings us to a second commitment every church should make, and that is to *send out missionaries.* The reason for this is very simple: There are still billions of people in the world who cannot be reached through friendship evangelism because none of their friends know the gospel. The spread of the gospel always requires an initial investment in cross-cultural evangelism, and this will continue to be the case for the foreseeable future.

There are many ways to spread the good news about Jesus Christ: evangelistic campaigns, Christian literature, evangelistic films, even the Internet. On occasion, short-term missionaries have opportunities to present the gospel, as well as to strengthen their own long-term commitment to support missions through prayer and giving. However, there is no substitute for personal, long-term, cross-cultural missionary work that establishes new churches in new places. We are called to make disciples, and discipleship demands relationships in which the love of Christ has a living presence. There is an incarnational aspect of evangelistic witness that requires person-to-person involvement. Our task is not simply to translate the Bible into every known language, or to give a basic gospel presentation to every tribe, or even to win converts from every ethnic group, but to communicate the Christian faith in all its fullness, so that people give their whole lives to God and to the service of His glory. The goal is to establish gospel-spreading churches that will perpetuate a church-planting movement within every people group. For so many unreached people in so many unreached places, this will never happen unless we go and give them the gospel.

Thankfully, Christianity seems to be spreading farther and faster than any other time in the last two thousand years. This is because Christians from Asia, Africa, and Latin America are beginning to mobilize for missions. But even as the church's center of gravity shifts away from the West, God is calling Americans to join an international partnership in reaching the world for Christ. This means sending out missionaries, and of course there are only missionaries to send if there are Christians who are willing to go. Personally, this is very costly, which no doubt explains why it is becoming so hard to recruit new missionaries. The only people who even consider becoming missionaries are people who are totally committed to living for Christ. And the only people who are totally committed to live for Christ are the ones who are willing to die for Christ.

I once asked a group of children in Sunday school how many of them wanted to live for Christ. Almost every hand went up. Then I asked them if they were willing to serve Christ "no matter what." Their hands stayed up until I asked, "How many of you are willing to die for Christ?" Most of the hands came down. I told them that until they were willing to die for Christ, they would not be able to live for Him, either—at least not the way that He wants them to live.

Jesus said that His followers would face deprivation and hardship. Are you willing to die and to live for Christ? Sadly, many Christians say to themselves, "I'm willing to do anything for God, as long as I don't have to become a missionary." Anyone who thinks this way really does not know what it means to be a Christian, because the first thing Jesus told His disciples was that they would have to give up everything to follow Him. This was essential because He was sending them on a dangerous mission. He was sending them to all nations, knowing that all nations would hate them, but also knowing that the nations needed His grace.

This is still true today. At this very moment there are people all over the world who have never heard the good news about Jesus Christ, and who therefore have never found their true joy in giving glory to God. Who will go and give them the gospel? Only those who are willing to pay the price. And unless we continue to send career missionaries, we will be guilty of the Great Omission—failing to help fulfill the mission that God has given His church for the world. What Jesus said to His disciples still sets the agenda for our prayers: "The harvest is plentiful but the workers are few. Ask the Lord of the harvest, therefore, to send out workers into his harvest field" (Matt. 9:37–38).

The third commitment every congregation should make is to *realize that every Christian is a missionary*. Although I have saved this point for last, it is really the most important, and perhaps the most neglected. Sadly, many churches view themselves more as "vendors of religious services and goods" than as "a body of people sent on a mission."[7] But when Jesus gave the Great Commission (Matt. 28:18–20; cf. John 17:18), He was not talking about something that some Christians do in some places; He was talking about what every Christian does in every place. Wherever you are, you have been sent on a mission. Your local community is your mission field. It is the place God has called you to stand, like a city on a hill.

For the Christian, missions is a way of life. Every Christian should be a world Christian, and every church should do its part in reaching the world for Christ. In America today, this means helping to plant growing, vibrant, missions-minded churches. It means re-evangelizing dying congregations by proclaiming the gospel all over again. It means reaching out to internationals, and thereby taking spiritual advantage of the continuous surge in U.S. immigration (legal and otherwise). It means seizing every appropriate opportunity to speak about spiritual things with friends, neighbors, co-workers, and family members.

Treating missions as a way of life also means penetrating society in culture-transforming ways. To say that every Christian is a missionary is not to say that every Christian should go into "full-time Christian work." Especially in these post-Christian times, America needs Christian lawyers and doctors, singers and dancers, builders and bakers, students and teachers, buyers and sellers, journalists and politicians. At every level of society and in every suitable occupation, Christians need to use their gifts in ways that honor God. The point here is not simply that Christians should witness on the job (although that is good to do whenever we have the chance), but that Christians should do their jobs in ways that allow God's will to make a difference in the world. Effective Christian participation in social institutions helps to influence the culture for Christ.

One way to learn how to be an everyday missionary is to follow the example of Christians who serve overseas. Most foreign missionaries correspond with their supporters. As I read what my missionary friends write in their e-mails and news-letters, I am often struck by how ordinary their work sounds. They ask me to pray for a colleague at work. They recount a conversation with a neighbor, in which they had the opportunity to speak about spiritual things. They describe the spiritual darkness in their local community. In other words, they write about the same kinds of things that I should be thinking about in my own neighborhood. Every Christian ought to consider himself or herself as a missionary. Who is the missionary in your apartment building, at your workplace, in your class, or on your softball team? You are.

Missions is not simply something that we support; it is who we are. If you're a Christian, you're a missionary. The only question is, How well are you doing your job? Whom are you loving, praying for, inviting to dinner, bringing to church? There is still a great deal of work to do—right here, right now, and all over the world, until Christ is preached to all nations. And then the end will come.

8

Serving with Compassion

✝

Mercy Ministry

In a book called *The Abandoned Generation,* William Willimon and Thomas Naylor of Duke University identify the priorities of the next generation of American college graduates. The results from a student survey taken at Duke's School of Business were especially telling. Students were asked, "What do you want to be when you grow up?" Willimon and Naylor write:

> With few exceptions, they wanted three things—money, power and things (very big things, including vacation homes, expensive foreign automobiles, yachts and even airplanes). Primarily concerned with their careers and the growth of their financial portfolios, their personal plans contained little room for family, intellectual development, spiritual growth or social responsibility. Their mandate to the faculty was, "Teach me how to be a

moneymaking machine." "Give me only the facts, tools and techniques required to ensure my instantaneous financial success." All else was irrelevant.[2]

Many Americans still seem to believe that the person who dies with the most toys wins. They would rather not be bothered with other people's pain and suffering. Some call it a "crisis of compassion." There was a time when Americans were known for helping one another out and for helping the world. We used to say, "Bring me your poor, your tired, your hungry." Now we often say, "Take them away! Take them somewhere else, so I don't have to worry about them or look after them. They can come back when they figure out how to solve their own problems." In these post-Christian times, most people pursue their own personal prosperity. They are too selfish to serve.

THE SHEEP AND THE GOATS

If it's true that the one who dies with the most toys wins, then it is important to make as much money as possible. However, that is not how God keeps score. His standard for judgment is based on servanthood. In the end, serving oneself rather than reaching out to others will prove to be a deadly mistake.

Jesus explained this by telling His disciples what would happen at the final judgment. What He told them was not so much a parable as a prophecy: "When the Son of Man comes in his glory, and all the angels with him, he will sit on his throne in heavenly glory. All the nations will be gathered before him, and he will separate the people one from another as a shepherd separates the sheep from the goats. He will put the sheep on his right and the goats on his left" (Matt. 25:31–33).

The scene would have been familiar to the disciples, for in those days separating the sheep from the goats was a common practice. The animals generally grazed together during the daytime, but when the weather was cool they were divided at nightfall. Goats are more sensitive to the cold; they need to huddle together. So Jesus and His disciples had often seen shepherds separate their sheep from their goats.

When night falls on human history, the separation will be permanent. On the one hand will be the sheep, whose lives were all about helping the weak:

> Then the King will say to those on his right, "Come, you who are blessed by my Father; take your inheritance, the kingdom prepared for you since the creation of the world. For I was hungry and you gave me something to eat, I was thirsty and you gave me something to drink, I was a stranger and you invited me in, I needed clothes and you clothed me, I was sick and you looked after me, I was in prison and you came to visit me."
>
> Then the righteous will answer him, "Lord, when did we see you hungry and feed you, or thirsty and give you something to drink? When did we see you a stranger and invite you in, or needing clothes and clothe you? When did we see you sick or in prison and go to visit you?"
>
> The King will reply, "I tell you the truth, whatever you did for one of the least of these brothers of mine, you did for me." (Matt. 25:34–40)

On God's other hand will be the goats, who never did anything in true service to Christ:

> Then he will say to those on his left, "Depart from me, you who are cursed, into the eternal fire prepared for the devil and his angels. For I was hungry and you gave me nothing to eat, I was thirsty and you gave me nothing to drink, I was a stranger

and you did not invite me in, I needed clothes and you did not clothe me, I was sick and in prison and you did not look after me."

They also will answer, "Lord, when did we see you hungry or thirsty or a stranger or needing clothes or sick or in prison, and did not help you?"

He will reply, "I tell you the truth, whatever you did not do for one of the least of these, you did not do for me."

Then they will go away to eternal punishment, but the righteous to eternal life. (Matt. 25:41–46)

This is one of the most sobering passages in the entire Bible. Jesus said these things to His disciples just three days before His betrayal, when He was already anticipating His sufferings and the way they would secure salvation for His people. But Jesus was also looking beyond the brutal cross to the final judgment, when "God will bring every deed into judgment, including every hidden thing, whether it is good or evil" (Eccles. 12:14).

The day of judgment will be full of surprises. Some people will be surprised that there will even *be* a judgment. All along they assumed that they could do whatever they pleased, instead of doing what God pleased. When they are finally held accountable for every selfish deed and every unkind word, it will come as a tremendous shock. Imagine how surprised the relativist will be when God applies an absolute moral standard to everything he ever did . . . and everything he decided not to do. And imagine how surprised the narcissist will be to discover that he is not the center of the universe after all. Judgment is coming, and many people will be surprised when it comes.

People will also be surprised to discover that Jesus will be their judge. When Jesus lived on this earth He was despised and rejected. He Himself was judged—tried according to the unfair standards of human justice, and then unlawfully executed. Yet the day is coming when Jesus will sit on God's throne and judge the nations, which is why it is so important for the nations to get the gospel. Every human being who has ever lived will stand for judgment. People think of Jesus as the suffering servant, or perhaps simply as a wise teacher, but now that He has offered satisfaction for sin, He is also the High King who rules the universe with perfect justice. Soon He will come in power and glory, attended by countless angels, to render universal judgment. He will sit down on God's throne to separate people for blessing and for cursing: this one to the kingdom of glory, that one to the fires of hell forever. Understand what this means: One day you personally will stand before Jesus for judgment. Are you ready to meet Him?

Here is another surprise: The standard that Jesus will apply is service to the hungry and the thirsty, the naked and the sick. As far as Jesus is concerned, whatever we do for the poor and needy—especially in the family of God—we are doing for Him. In effect, Jesus said, "I am the starving child, the homeless man, the outsider, the invalid, the inmate." This will come as a surprise to those who are saved. They will say, "Jesus, when did we ever feed You, clothe You, or visit You?" They will be surprised, not so much by their salvation, but by how important it was for them to do something they could hardly even remember doing: showing mercy to seemingly insignificant others.

The goats will be even more surprised. They will be surprised by God's sentence against their sin: "Depart from me, you who are cursed, into the eternal fire" (Matt. 25:41). They will also be surprised by the reason for this fearful verdict. They were always busy taking care of their own business and pursuing their own pleasures. It never even occurred to them that it mattered how they treated "the little people." But Jesus will say to them, "Whatever you did not do for one of the least of these, you did not do for me" (Matt. 25:45). If they had known it was

Jesus, why, of course they would have done something to help! But it was Jesus all along, and in the end, they will be cursed for their sins of omission: They never did anything for Jesus.

Finally, the goats will be surprised by the length of their sentence, for "they will go away to eternal punishment" (Matt. 25:46). Some theologians take issue with the biblical doctrine of endless torment, but when it comes to the pains of hell, and to their duration, Jesus was never a relativist. In fact, a large proportion of the biblical teaching about eternal damnation comes directly from Jesus. Here, by giving His disciples the symbolic prophecy of the sheep and the goats, He was saying, "I promise you, mercy is a matter of eternal life and death."

SAVED BY WORKS?

In His prophecy Jesus mentioned a half dozen merciful deeds—what the early church called "the six acts of charity": feeding the hungry, satisfying the thirsty, welcoming the stranger, clothing the naked, caring for the sick, and visiting the prisoner. In some way these good deeds are all connected to salvation. This often troubles Christians who know that salvation is by grace, and not by works. If we are saved by what Christ has done, rather than by what we can do, then why did Jesus make charity the standard for entering His glory? In this prophecy He says nothing about faith; it is all about works. Nor is there any mention of the cross and the empty tomb.

There are many ways to deal with this difficulty. One is to point out that what Jesus said about the sheep and the goats needs to be interpreted in the light of everything else the Bible says about salvation. Whatever this prophecy means, it does not contradict the biblical message of salvation by grace alone, through faith alone, in Christ alone. At the beginning of his gospel, Matthew announced that Jesus "will save his people from their sins" (Matt. 1:21). Obviously, the prophecy He reports at the end of the same gospel is not intended to teach that we can save ourselves by showing kindness to strangers. Here it is especially important to remember everything else the Bible says about what God has done for His sheep. The sheep God saves at the final judgment are the same ones He found when they were lost (Luke 15:3–7) and for whom Christ laid down His life (John 10:11).

Another way to answer the question of works righteousness is to show that even in this passage eternal life is a gift of divine grace rather than a reward for human merit. There are several indications of this. For one thing, Jesus will invite His sheep to receive His kingdom as an inheritance (Matt. 25:34). But an inheritance is never earned; it always comes as a gift. So even before Jesus said anything about the six acts of charity, He welcomed the righteous into glory as a legacy of His grace. Furthermore, they were chosen for this salvation before the beginning of time. At the judgment Jesus will say to His sheep, "Come, you who are blessed by my Father; take your inheritance, the kingdom prepared for you since the creation of the world" (Matt. 25:34). The favor of God the Father has rested on these sheep from all eternity. Their salvation is not based on justification by works; rather, it rests on election by grace.

It is also important to understand the precise meaning of the word "for" (Matt. 25:35), which connects the sheep entering heaven with their righteous deeds on earth. It is often assumed here that "for" means "because," so that Jesus was saying, in effect, "Come to heaven *because* you fed Me and cared for Me." In that case, the six acts of charity would provide the meritorious basis for eternal life. However, the word "for" is not always causal; sometimes it is evidential. In other words, it shows *that* something happened without necessarily explaining why, or on what basis. Consider the following sentences: "The homeless are not hungry today, for the church has supplied their need"; "The homeless are not hungry today, for they are not coming in to eat dinner." The first sentence explains the logical cause for the event in question: The homeless are not hungry because they have been fed. The second sentence simply provides evidence from which it can be inferred that the homeless aren't hungry, without indicating why.

To apply the example, when Jesus used the word "for" to connect glory with charity ("Come, take your inheritance, for I was hungry"), He was giving the evidence for His people's salvation rather than explaining its cause. Jesus was not teaching salvation by works. We do not present good deeds to God as our righteousness, but as the fruit of our faith. Our works will either provide evidence of God's gracious work in our lives or they will prove that we have rejected that grace. At the final judgment, our relationship to Christ will be revealed by what we have done—or failed to do—for Him.

One more detail helps confirm that the prophecy of the sheep and the goats is not intended to teach that salvation can be earned by performing good works. Notice why the sheep are surprised. They are not surprised to be received into glory. They do not ask, "Lord, why are You letting us into heaven?" They know Jesus Christ, and thus they obtained assurance of their salvation long ago. What surprises them is that Jesus brings up their good deeds at all. This makes it obvious that they have not been working for their salvation. In that case, they would have said something like, "Thank You, Lord, we've been hoping You'd notice what we did." Instead, they are totally surprised that Jesus makes any connection at all between their good works and their glorious inheritance. That being the case, Jesus could hardly want us to conclude from this prophecy that helping the poor is the way for us to earn our salvation!

CHARITY IN SIX ACTS

These clarifications are necessary. It is important to understand that the prophecy of the sheep and the goats does not teach salvation by works. However, it is possible to spend so much time explaining what the prophecy doesn't mean that we miss what it *does* mean. What it means is that God wants us to show active compassion through service, because this is one of the surest signs that we have been saved by His grace. How we treat the poor and needy indicates where we stand with God Himself. If we don't care to have a relationship with God, we won't care very much about the needs of the poor. However, if we love God, then we will prove it by loving the least and the lost, for Jesus' sake. Indeed, showing mercy is such an essential mark of being a Christian that Jesus can and will use it as one test of genuine faith.

Jesus taught about the sheep and the goats to help us understand our responsibility as agents of His mercy. The prophecy makes some people nervous. Somewhat understandably, they worry whether they will be taken to heaven or banished to hell. Presumably Jesus intended His prophecy to have precisely this effect. When He came to the end, He did not say to His disciples, "Look, I know that all this talk of eternal punishment is a little unsettling, but don't worry about it, because I'm going to forgive you anyway." On the contrary, Jesus wanted to be sure His disciples knew that they would have to account for their works. He also wanted to give them the strongest incentive to serve. Therefore, He told them that mercy was a matter of life and death. Acts of charity are not optional; they are at the very heart of what it means to be a servant of Jesus Christ. This is because, as it says in the mission statement of Bethel Baptist Church in Minneapolis, "the all-satisfying supremacy of God shines most brightly through sacrificial deeds of joyful love."

The six acts of charity have several things in common. To begin with, they all concern physical needs. Food and water are basic human needs. When these needs go unmet, people die from starvation and dehydration. The stranger needs a place to stay. There were no motels in biblical times, so travelers depended on the kindness of strangers. Otherwise, they were exposed to the elements and sometimes to personal violence. The naked need clothes; not having them is a sign of extreme poverty. The sick need medical attention to nurse them back to health. Prisoners need the most help of all. Prisons were grim places in the time of Christ, and many inmates depended on friends to bring them food, water, and clothing.

Meeting such physical needs requires a personal investment, which is something else these deeds have in common. A material investment has to be made. It takes money and other resources to give food, to house guests, and to buy clothes. But the investment is also spiritual. It is impossible to care for the needy without knowing who they are, what they need, and how they should be helped. This takes time to figure out. It also takes wisdom, so that instead of always dealing with immediate needs, the deepest spiritual needs of the poor are discerned and addressed. In short, offering mercy means having a relationship that leads from poverty to responsibility. Usually this is the difference between good charity and bad charity. Bad charity throws money at a problem without getting personally involved, with the result that the underlying causes of problems like poverty and homelessness are never dealt with. Good charity makes a total commitment to meeting someone's total needs.

Here is another commonality: All six acts of charity are offered to what Jesus called "the least," in other words, to people who would otherwise go neglected. He said, "I tell you the truth, whatever you did for one of the least of these brothers of mine, you did for me" (Matt. 25:40). Jesus gives special significance to those who seem unimportant (especially our brothers and sisters in the faith, which as we shall see is what Jesus specifically meant by "the least of these brothers of mine").

God's special concern for the disadvantaged runs right through the Bible: "There will always be poor people in the land. Therefore I command you to be openhanded toward your brothers and toward the poor and needy in your land" (Deut. 15:11). "He will deliver the needy who cry out, the afflicted who have no one to help. He will take pity on the weak and the needy and save the needy from death" (Ps. 72:12–13). "Religion that God our Father accepts as pure and faultless is this: to look after orphans and widows in their distress" (James 1:27). These passages are typical of God's compassion for the underprivileged.

Given this background, it is not surprising that the true test for God's servants is how they treat people whom nobody wants, nobody loves, and nobody touches because they just can't seem to get their act together. Who really cares about the homeless? Or about immigrants who can't speak English? Or about sick, lonely people languishing in a nursing home? Or about people dying from AIDS? Or about criminals locked up in prison? God does, and so should all His servants.

FOR JESUS' SAKE

There are many reasons to perform the six acts of charity. The most obvious is the simple fact that these good deeds badly need to be done. Food, clothing, medicine—these are basic human needs that still must be met in the twenty-first century. People are starving. Nations are ravaged by war. Most Third World countries have an urgent need for medical care. Natural disasters routinely cause great suffering in various places around the world, especially for those who lose their homes. But even in the United States of America, there are many homeless who need a good meal and a safe place to sleep. One out of five American children lives below the poverty line. This is an age of immigration, with people moving to this country from all over the world. There is a tremendous need for them to receive education and other practical assistance. Then there is America's rapidly growing prison population, with nearly two million inmates locked behind bars. The needs have never been greater than in these post-Christian times.

There are many reasons that the church should get involved in meeting these needs. There is the simple fact that God has commanded us to have compassion on the needy. Then there is the strategic importance of showing mercy to reach the next generation. Many young people want to make a difference in the world. Unless they see the church demonstrating mercy and compassion in practical ways, they will not listen to our message —nor should they. But a church that is committed to outreach offers them a place to belong, and, eventually, a place to serve. The church should also show mercy because it confirms the truth of God's Word. The Bible is sufficient to bring salvation. However, when the Word of truth is accompanied by a work of mercy, the powerful, living demonstration of Christ's love has the effect of turning up the volume on the gospel.

Those are all good reasons to show mercy, but Jesus pointed to something else. In His teaching on the sheep and goats, He gave the purest and truest motive for mercy. He said, "Do it for Me." The righteous do not perform the six acts of charity in order to get to heaven. No, what makes their service supremely valuable is that they offer it for Jesus' sake. Love for the poor and the needy expresses true love for Christ.

Why would anyone love Christ so much? It is because He first showed His love to us. One of the striking things about the six acts of charity is that they are all things that Jesus has done and continues to do for His sheep. The mercy we give is the mercy we have been given.

We are hungry and thirsty. In our spiritual famine, Jesus comes to us and says, "I am the bread of life. He who comes to me will never go hungry" (John 6:35). In our thirst for spiritual refreshment, He says, "If anyone is thirsty, let him come to me and drink" (John 7:37). There was a time when we were estranged from God by our sin. The Bible says, "Once you were alienated from God and were enemies in your minds because of your evil behavior. But now he has reconciled you by Christ's physical body through death" (Col. 1:21–22a). Through the cross of Christ, God has shown us the hospitality of His grace, turning us from strangers into friends.

What about clothes for the naked? The Bible often uses clothing imagery to describe our salvation. God covers the shameful nakedness of our sin with the beautiful robes of Christ's righteousness. So the Scripture says, "Clothe yourselves with the Lord Jesus Christ" (Rom. 13:14). Jesus is also the remedy for our sin-sick souls. He came "healing every disease and sickness" (Matt. 4:23), and saying, "It is not the healthy who need a doctor, but the sick" (Matt. 9:12). The final act of charity is to visit those who are in prison, but Jesus does more than just visit. He comes "to proclaim freedom for the prisoners" (Luke 4:18), breaking the chains of sin. The six acts of charity thus describe six aspects of salvation. Jesus feeds the hungry, satisfies the thirsty, welcomes the stranger, clothes the naked, heals the sick, and sets the captive free.

At the end of history, when the entire human race gathers before God's throne, Jesus will say to His friends, "Come into My kingdom. I know you belong because you showed Me mercy." They will be astonished to hear this, and so they will ask, "When did we show You mercy?" Jesus will say, "When you did it for them, you were doing it for Me." Then perhaps we will be able to say, "Jesus, the only reason we did it for them was because You did it for us first." *This is why a church for the twenty-first century serves its congregation and its community through ministries of mercy: It is because we have been saved by a merciful God.*

HAVE MERCY!

Every Christian and every church should be active in some form of mercy ministry. Mercy always begins at home, so our first priority is to meet the needs of our own family—meaning both our natural family and our spiritual family, which is the church. The Bible teaches that our strongest obligation is to care for those who are closest to us: "If anyone does not provide for his relatives, and especially for his immediate family, he has denied the faith and is worse than an unbeliever" (I Tim. 5:8). The same principle holds true for the church: "As we have opportunity, let us do good to all people, especially to those who belong to the family of believers" (Gal. 6:10; cf. I Thess. 3:12; James 2; I John 3:17–18).

We find the same emphasis in the prophecy of the sheep and the goats, in which Jesus refers to "the least of these brothers of mine" (Matt. 25:40). Both the word "least" and the word "brothers" are used elsewhere in Matthew's gospel with specific reference to the followers of Christ.[3] So Jesus is referring most specifically to the way we care for His followers. The test of our love for Christ is compassion for other Christians.

This is the special work of the deacons, who have carried out servant ministry since the earliest days of the church. When the apostles found that caring for the poor was distracting them from their primary callings of preaching and prayer, they set apart spiritual men to oversee the daily distribution of food (Acts 6:1–7). Out of this division of labor grew the office of deacon, a ministry of service to the church. Deacons have the privilege of offering spiritual counsel and practical assistance in the context of physical need. In addition to doing practical things like looking after the church's physical property and assisting with the logistics of worship, their work may include meal preparation, child care, transportation, hospitality, home repairs, financial counseling, monetary assistance, and everything else that meets a practical need. But while mercy is the special work of deacons, it is also the work of every Christian. Whenever we hear that someone in the church has a need, we should ask if there is anything we can do to help. This is one of the reasons it is so important to be involved in a smaller group somewhere in the church. As we saw back in chapter 4, we need to know people well enough to know their needs and be able to help meet them.

Although charity begins at home, that is not where it stops. Through faith in Jesus Christ, we are connected to Christians all over the world, and we ought to have compassion for their needs. Because they are our brothers and sisters in Christ, they have a special claim on our pity. This means paying for disaster relief, assisting with community development, praying for the persecuted church, and sending missionaries equipped with practical skills to meet physical needs. By doing these things, we show the mercy of Christ.

Finally, we must care for our surrounding community. Although this is not the primary focus of Matthew 25, it is an obvious extension of its principles. In an attempt to summarize the biblical teaching about mercy at home and abroad, Timothy Keller offers the following guidelines: "As a priority, we should give to needy Christians both intensively and extensively, until their need is gone. But we must also give generously to nonbelievers as part of our witness to the world. . . . In other words, the ministry of mercy is not only an expression of the *fellowship* of the church, but also an expression of the *mission* of the church."[4] To put this another way, charity should not be kept in the family; it is also for neighbors and strangers.

In the same way that Jesus reached out to us, we must reach out to the hungry, the thirsty, the stranger, the naked, the sick, and the prisoner. This means reaching out to international students, unwed mothers, homosexuals, people with AIDS, the elderly, inner city children, the jobless, the homeless, the separated and divorced, single parents, the disabled, and the imprisoned. In each of these and many other areas of human need, church members should be on the lookout for people who could use some help, and then under the direction of their pastors, elders, and deacons, organize themselves for effective ministry. This is what mercy requires: both the identification of a need and a personal commitment to meet that need in the compassion of Christ.

Compassion has become something of a political slogan, but what it actually requires is a costly personal commitment to befriend the poor and needy. Offering true mercy is one of the things that ought to distinguish the church from the world. Rather than trying to be as much like the world as possible, our goal is to be like Jesus Christ. Among other things, this means that we are called to be radically different in giving the gift of mercy.

In 1992 Marvin Olasky wrote an influential book called *The Tragedy of American Compassion.*[5] Simply stated, Olasky's thesis was that bad charity drives out good charity. Good charity offers practical assistance, but at the same time it requires personal accountability. It is the kind of ministry churches can provide by encouraging long-term spiritual change, instead of simply offering short-term help. Bad charity is the kind government programs too often provide: a handout without a hand up. In other words, although material assistance is provided, nothing is done to foster a sense of individual responsibility or to address the structural causes of poverty. Olasky makes a persuasive case for returning to good charity, but this requires active Christian involvement in meeting local needs. My fear is that we have grown so used to depending on the government to solve social problems that we no longer have the skills or the interest to reach out. Call it the tragedy of Christian compassion: an unwillingness to make a costly investment in caring for others and dealing with their misfortunes.

The twenty-first century will bring new opportunities for Christian individuals, households, and churches to demonstrate active compassion through service. It is impossible to predict what kinds of hardship people will face here in America and around the world. Undoubtedly hardships will come from natural disasters, acts of terror, and the unjust structures of a sinful society. In many cases the needs will be acute, the sufferings will be intense, and the victims will be unprepared for the miseries they face. In order to fulfill our calling to meet these challenges, standing like a city on a hill, we must be mobilized to minister with the mercy of Christ.

London's Mark Greene has written a poem about offering mercy. Written for postmodern times, the poem presents a popular version of chaos theory, the scientific idea that a small change in one part of the world can trigger a chain of events that ultimately produces a major change somewhere else. It begins like this:

> *With a tremor of its wafer wing,*
> *They say, a butterfly in Beijing*
> *Can, in time, spin a tornado*
> *across the Kansas plain,*
> *Or hurl a tidal wave booming into Carolina's tranquil bays.*

Then Greene draws a comparison to show how an act of mercy can change the world:

> *So, what then of a kiss for the dying,*
> *An embrace for the untouched,*
> *Or a tenderness to the crushed?*
>
> *What of a whisper of grace,*
> *A word of love unfurled,*
> *Or a door to truth flung wide?*
>
> *Will not these unwind the twisted heart*
> *And still the waves of endless whys?*
> *Is this not the fountain spray*
> *That soars through time*
> *And splashes eternity in our eyes?*[6]

The answer is yes. By serving with compassion we show Christ's mercy to the world—the love that not only touches the broken body, but heals the wounded heart.

9

Why the Church
Needs the Gospel

✝

Repentance and Renewal

> *"Slippage in our consciousness of sin, like most fashionable follies, may be pleasant, but it is also devastating. Self-deception about our sin is a narcotic, a tranquilizing and disorienting suppression of our spiritual central nervous system."*
>
> —↶ CORNELIUS PLANTINGA, JR.

This book began with the claim that we are living in post-Christian times. By all accounts, the evangelical church is in decline, and so is American culture. At the start of the twenty-first century the Bible is considered largely irrelevant to public life. Sometimes its adherents are even considered dangerous. Witness the current bumper sticker: "God, Save Me From Your Followers."

Christianity no longer shapes the social, political, and moral landscape of our nation the way it once did. Other forces are at work. Although there are many ways to analyze what's wrong with American culture, two of the biggest culprits are relativism and narcissism. Relativism is extreme skepticism, the denial that there is any such thing as absolute truth. It is the mind-set that led a housewife from Dayton, Ohio, to say, "Nothing is black and white and every circumstance merits its own judgment."[1] Narcissism is extreme individualism, the demand for absolute individual autonomy. It is self-admiration, self-satisfaction, self-glorification. It was the narcissist who said, "I believe everybody should really be able to basically do what they want to do."[2]

A CHURCH FOR THE TWENTY-FIRST CENTURY

In these relativistic, narcissistic times, some Christians say that we need to find a new way of doing church. We are facing new challenges that require a new response. So we should change the style of our preaching, worship, outreach, architecture—possibly even our message—anything to attract the interest of lost and dying people in a lost and dying culture.

This book has offered an alternative approach, not for the sake of tradition, but in order to discern what is timeless and true. Rather than asking what our culture wants, we started by asking what the Bible teaches. To live for Christ in post-Christian times, the church must embrace a thoroughly biblical model for everything it does. To this end, a church for the twenty-first century:

- upholds a tradition of strong expository preaching by gifted men of God;
- worships God in a worthy manner through thoughtful words, devoted prayers, and excellent music;
- integrates every member of the congregation into Bible studies and other groups where individual needs can be met and each can minister to others;
- supplies loving pastoral care for each member of the church family;
- provides an effective Christian education program to inform, train, and disciple all members of the congregation;

- advances the missionary work of the church in the local community and throughout the world; and
- serves its congregation and its community through ministries of mercy.

This is the biblical pattern for the church. However, it also proves to be exactly the kind of church that is needed for the twenty-first century. One reason for this is that the Bible is God's answer to the problems of relativism and narcissism. It is not surprising, therefore, that a church based on the Bible is perfectly suited to proclaim the gospel in post-Christian times. At every time and in every place, the church that is best equipped to meet people's spiritual needs is a biblical church.

How does the church respond to relativism? It starts with biblical teaching, with making God's Word plain in an evangelical, doctrinal, and practical way. The standard of biblical authority is preserved and protected by the church's elders, who are the shepherds of God's flock. Relativism is also countered by a biblical approach to missions and evangelism, in which Jesus Christ is presented as the only way to God. Expository preaching, pastoral care, world missions—these priorities help the church promote God's unchanging truth in changing times.

At the same time, the biblical pattern for the church helps preserve us from becoming self-centered, despite the fact that we live in a culture of narcissism. God-centered worship shifts attention away from what we want to what God wants, so that the goal becomes pleasing God with our praise. Within our fellowship we use our gifts to care for others, not to serve ourselves. Then, in gratitude to God for His great love, we extend the mercy of Christ to those who are outside the church.

In order to do all this effectively, we must pay the cost of discipleship. Thus a church for post-Christian times is a countercultural community that stands for God and His truth, rather than for me and my agenda. It is the alternative spiritual society in which we learn not to live for ourselves, but to die to the world and all it seems to offer. In their book *Resident Aliens*, Stanley Hauerwas and William Willimon argue that the way the church influences the world is

> by being the church, that is, by being something the world is not and can never be, lacking the gift of faith and vision, which is ours in Christ. The confessing church seeks the visible church, a place, clearly visible to the world, in which people are faithful to their promises, love their enemies, tell the truth, honor the poor, suffer for righteousness, and thereby testify to the amazing community-creating power of God. . . . The church knows that its most credible form of witness (and the most "effective" thing it can do for the world) is the actual creation of a living, breathing, visible community of faith.[3]

NOT THE WAY IT'S SUPPOSED TO BE

The problem is that the world is too much with us, and so the church is too much like the world. Christians are fast becoming as relativistic and narcissistic as anyone else. Even non-Christians have started to notice. *The New Yorker*, of all places, complains: "The preacher, instead of looking out upon the world, looks out on public opinion, trying to find out what the public would like to hear. Then he tries his best to duplicate that, and bring his finished product into a marketplace in which others are trying to do the same. The public, turning to our church culture to find out about the world, discovers there is nothing but its own reflection."[4] Of course then the question becomes, Why even bother to go to church?

The sad truth is that in each and every area of ministry, the church is crippled by its sin. Start with expository preaching.

The ministry of God's Word is often hindered by the minister. Sometimes in his disobedience he does not really listen to what it says. Sometimes he preaches without courage, for fear of opposition. Sometimes he preaches without love, for lack of compassion. When one of my colleagues telephones other congregations, he sometimes asks to speak to "the biggest sinner in the church." He means, of course, the pastor. This may seem mischievous, but it has the serious purpose of showing that ministers need the gospel at least as much as anyone else.

Now consider a church's fellowship, and all of the ways it is hindered by envy, discord, gossip, selfishness, and strife. We are quick to take offense, but slow to forgive. We are more interested in having our own gifts recognized than in honoring the gifts of others. And of course this is only the beginning. In our worship we are guilty of sinful thoughts and irreverent attitudes. In our pastoral care we are negligent and inconsistent. In our discipleship we often take the easy way out. In our missions and evangelism we lack passion for the lost and zeal for God's glory. Our outreach to the needy is constrained by our lack of mercy. As Jesus taught us to say, "We are unworthy servants" (Luke 17:10).

When I speak of the church's failures, I am not talking about someone else's church, I am talking about my own. A woman from Tenth Presbyterian Church wrote:

> We are blind to our worldliness partly because it seems normal and true. Lately I have been realizing in new ways how insidious the influence of the world is. Our sense of identity, our values, and even our understanding of history are drastically skewed by worldliness. . . . Although as Christians we claim to renounce the love of the world, the superficiality of our faith allows us to blind ourselves to our hearts' idolatry of worldliness. For many of us, although we like to think we are allowing God to transform us and renew our minds, the transformation is only superficial. There

remains a major disconnect between what we believe in our heads and what we feel to be true deep down in our hearts. And our actions are usually motivated by the underlying idols and twisted truth in our hearts. We don't examine ourselves deeply enough to let the light of God's truth penetrate those dark places at the core of our being. Instead we just try to fix the symptoms of the problem . . . but never address the sinful desires and warped thinking which cause them. We hide our idols and our wounds so well that we are able to deceive ourselves that they don't exist.[5]

This is why the church needs the gospel. It is because we are full of sin—absolutely full of it. Look at any congregation on any given Sunday, and you will see row upon row of twisted, hardened sinners who love the world more than they ever loved Christ.

IF WE CONFESS OUR SINS

It is impossible to understand what it means to be a city on a hill without being brutally honest about our sin. This is something the apostle John tried to do in his first epistle, which he began by explaining why the church needs the gospel.

In those days certain Bible teachers denied the totality of their depravity. John made three statements to summarize their mistaken theology, each of which began with the words, "If we claim . . .":

"If we claim to have fellowship with him yet walk in the darkness, we lie and do not live by the truth" (I John 1:6).

"If we claim to be without sin, we deceive ourselves and the truth is not in us" (I John 1:8).

"If we claim we have not sinned, we make him out to be a liar and his word has no place in our lives" (1 John 1:10).

In one way or another, each of these claims denies the biblical doctrine of sin. The first one (verse 6) denies that sin affects our relationship with God, as if we could lead a life characterized by habitual ungodliness and still have unbroken fellowship with God. Anyone who operates this way is living a lie. The claim in verse 8 denies our sinful nature. It asserts that we are basically good; in our essence as human beings, we are without sin. Anyone who thinks this way is self-deceived. The last claim (verse 10) denies having committed any particular sins at all. Notice the past tense: "have not sinned." Here the claim is not simply that it is not our nature to sin, but that in fact we have never actually committed any sins. This is a deliberate lie because everyone knows that everyone sins.

The basic theological error in all three of these statements is perfectionism, the belief that it is possible to be sinless in the present life. The apostle John was responding to Christians who thought they had it all together, and who therefore failed to recognize that they needed the gospel as much as anyone else. Understand that the gospel is not something we believe when we first become Christians and then outgrow; it is something we need every moment of every day. The reason is that we are *not* without sin. We never have been and we never will be, until we get to glory.

Instead of denying the pervasive power and presence of sin, the thing to do is to confess it. Here is another one of John's "if" statements: "If we confess our sins, he is faithful and just and will forgive us our sins and purify us from all unrighteousness" (1 John 1:9). Sin is not to be denied; it is to be confessed. Rather than claiming that we are perfect, we must admit that we are corrupt to the very core. Not only are we naughty by nature, but we have also committed many actual sins.

If we are to be forgiven, then our sins must be confessed, not only personally, but also corporately. Repentance should be part of the rhythm of congregational life. A Christian church for post-Christian times confesses its failure to honor God in all seven of the priorities advocated in this book. Since we sin in every area, we must also seek forgiveness in every area, saying:

> Great God in heaven, we have sinned. We confess that we do not truly listen to Your Word. We read it and hear it, but we do not obey it. We say, "That was a great sermon!" but it doesn't make much difference, because we are not willing to change.
>
> We confess that we do not worship You the way You deserve to be worshiped. We are more concerned about what we get out of it than what we put into it. We are often distracted. Our lips keep moving, but our hearts are cold and still.
>
> We confess that we do not love one another very much. We do not want to be bothered with other people's problems. We do not care enough to confront, but when other Christians fail, we are quick to condemn them. We think the worst about others, rather than the best.
>
> We confess that we do not always fulfill our responsibilities to one another. Those of us who are shepherds have little love for Your sheep. We are harsh when we should be gentle, and when we need to be firm, we lack the courage to say or do what is right. Those of us who are sheep do not honor our shepherds. We fail to pray for them, and then we complain when they do not meet our expectations.
>
> We confess that we are not willing to pay the high cost of discipleship. We try to be as worldly as we think we can get away with. We prefer to squeeze our faith in around the edges of life, rather than to let You stand at the center to control everything we are and have.

We confess that we lack passion for missions and evangelism. We think of missions as something someone else does, somewhere else, rather than something You have called us to do right here and now. We lack the courage to proclaim the gospel. We are afraid to talk about spiritual things, for fear of what our friends may think.

We confess that we lack compassion. We think it is important to help the poor, provided that someone else actually does the helping.

In the name of Jesus, we ask forgiveness for these and all our sins. Amen.

HE WILL FORGIVE OUR SINS

What happens when we confess our sins? It is very simple: "If we confess our sins, he is faithful and just and will forgive us our sins and purify us from all unrighteousness" (1 John 1:9). God has promised to forgive everyone who truly seeks His forgiveness. He offers a total pardon that extends to each and every sin, including sins committed by people in the church, who ought to know better. And this promise comes with the promise of purification. By the sanctifying ministry of His Spirit, God is working to make us clean.

Earlier we noted three "if" statements that deny the reality of sin. Each of them is also followed by an "if" statement—not to deny sin, but to deal with it:

"If we walk in the light, as he is in the light, we have fellowship with one another, and the blood of Jesus, his Son, purifies us from all sin" (1 John 1:7).

"If we confess our sins, he is faithful and just and will forgive us our sins and purify us from all unrighteousness" (1 John 1:9).

"If anybody does sin, we have one who speaks to the Father in our defense—Jesus Christ, the Righteous One. He is the atoning sacrifice for our sins" (1 John 2:1b–2a).

What these statements have in common is that they all point to salvation in Christ. God's answer to the problem of our sin is the gospel, the good news about Jesus. The first statement speaks of "the blood of Jesus" (1 John 1:7). This refers to the lifeblood that He shed on the cross. The blood of Jesus, which paid the price for sin, has the power to purify, in other words, to remove the guilty stain of our sin.

The second statement speaks of God's justice. God does not simply overlook our sin. Indeed, He cannot. He is a righteous God, and therefore it would not be right for Him to forgive us, unless in some way our sin received the penalty it deserves. But God has preserved His justice by receiving the punishment for our sin in the person of His own Son. It is on this basis that "he is faithful and just and will forgive us our sins" (1 John 1:9).

The third statement identifies Jesus as "the atoning sacrifice" (1 John 2:2). To use the proper term for it—the English term that accurately translates the original Greek—Jesus is our *propitiation.* To propitiate is to turn away wrath. The fact that propitiation is needed shows how much God hates our sin. Unless His anger is turned aside, we will be destroyed by the holiness of His justice. But Jesus has propitiated God's wrath. He has done this by offering Himself as a perfectly righteous sacrifice for our sin.

This does not mean that God the Son had to persuade God the Father to love us, even though He didn't want to. On the contrary, making atonement for sin was the Father's idea in the first place. As John wrote near the end of his letter, "This is how God showed his love among us: He sent his one and only

Son into the world that we might live through him. This is love: not that we loved God, but that he loved us and sent his Son as an atoning sacrifice for our sins" (1 John 4:9–10). Making propitiation was the Father's loving plan. The Cross was God's way of turning aside His own wrath.

To summarize, God offers forgiveness for sin through the person and work of Jesus Christ—specifically through His death on the cross. This is something that Jesus did in the past: He died on the cross to atone for sin. That part of His saving work is finished. However, in order for us to be forgiven, we also need Jesus to do something for us now. We need Him to take His atoning work and apply it directly to our sins. God has made provision for the forgiveness of our sin through the present work of Jesus Christ. John wrote, "If anybody does sin, we have one who speaks to the Father in our defense— Jesus Christ, the Righteous One" (1 John 2:1b).

In one sense, Christ's work is finished. He paid full price for sin on the cross; no further payment is needed. However, Jesus continues to take what He has already done for our salvation and to give it to us today. To describe this ongoing work, John uses a term that comes from a court of law: Jesus "speaks to the Father in our defense." That is to say, He is our advocate, our legal counsel, our defense attorney. Jesus Christ stands before the most supreme of all courts to present His work on the cross as the basis for our forgiveness.

It is all too easy to criticize the church. After all, it is made up entirely of sinners, so it is never hard to find someone or something to complain about. Satan specializes in this kind of thing. He is always busy accusing us for our sins. But no matter what Satan or anyone else says about us, Jesus is always ready and able to defend us. He constantly intercedes on behalf of His church. He does not claim that we are not guilty; He must speak the truth about us, acknowledging that we are sinners.

However, He presents His saving work as our airtight defense against every accusation. Whenever there is any question about our standing before God, Jesus points back to the cross, where He atoned for our sin. "Who is he that condemns? Christ Jesus, who died—more than that, who was raised to life—is at the right hand of God and is also interceding for us" (Rom. 8:34). This is what Jesus is doing at this very moment: defending us so that we will receive the forgiveness He has promised.

Jesus intercedes for us in all our failures. He intercedes for preachers who, through their own weakness and sin, distort the truth of God's Word. He intercedes for the worshipers who have lost their passion for God's glory. He intercedes for Christians who disturb the peace of the church or who are too selfish to serve. He intercedes for missionaries who have decided to give up their calling. Jesus stands before His Father's throne and says, "Yes, it's all true. They are guilty as charged. But may it please the Court to remember that I have died for their sins."

No one knows how many problems there are in the church any better than Jesus does. He sees it all, which is why His ministry of intercession is a full-time job. The Bible teaches that "he is able to save completely those who come to God through him, because he always lives to intercede for them" (Heb. 7:25). Therefore, the church that always needs the gospel always *has* the gospel. If we trust in Jesus, then no matter how badly we make a mess of things, He is always rising to our defense, presenting His atoning, propitiating work as the forgiveness for our sins.

GATHERED BY GRACE

As a pastor, I am often amazed that the church is able to do anything good at all. I really mean this. The sins I know about are shocking enough, but there are many more sins that have never been discovered. We are so desperately sinful that it is remarkable God is able to use us to convert anyone, or to help anyone grow in the knowledge of Jesus Christ. We have only one saving grace: the grace that God has given us in the gospel of His Son.

Mark Noll has written a wonderful poem about the church's need for the gospel, and about the way the gospel meets that need. The poem—called "Scots' Form in the Suburbs"—is based on the old Scottish practice of gathering around tables for communion. According to the Scottish form of celebrating the sacrament, rather than having the elements distributed row by row, or kneeling before an altar, church members walk to the front of the church and sit down at the Lord's Table in groups.

Noll describes a church full of sinners going forward to share communion:

> *The sedentary Presbyterians*
> *awoke, arose, and filed to tables spread*
> *with white, to humble bits that showed how God*
> *Almighty had decided to embrace*
> *humanity, and why these clean, well-fed,*
> *well-dressed suburbanites might need his grace.*

Then the poet describes what these people are really like, on the inside:

> *The pious cruel, the petty gossipers*
> *and callous climbers on the make, the wives*
> *with icy tongues and husbands with their hearts*
> *of stone, the ones who battle drink and do*
> *not always win, the power lawyers mute*
> *before this awful bar of mercy, boys*
> *uncertain of themselves and girls not sure*
> *of where they fit, the poor and rich hemmed in*

alike by cash, physicians waiting to
be healed, two women side by side——the one
with unrequited longing for a child,
the other terrified by signs within
of life, the saintly weary weary in
pursuit of good, the academics (soft
and cosseted) who posture with their words,
the travelers coming home from chasing wealth
or power or wantonness, the mothers choked
by dual duties, parents nearly crushed
by children died or lost, and some
with cancer-ridden bodies, some with spikes
of pain in chest or back or knee or mind
or heart. They come, O Christ, they come to you.

The poem closes by explaining what grace this motley band of sinners received:

They came, they sat, they listened to the words,
"for you my body broken." Then they ate
and turned away——the spent unspent, the dead
recalled, a hint of color on the psychic
cheek——from tables groaning under weight
of tiny cups and little crumbs of bread.[6]

I understand the poem well because I used to be a member of the very local church Dr. Noll described in his poem. And I am in need of the same grace. But really, the same collection of sinners is found in every congregation. In the whole history of Christianity, there has never been a church that did not need the gospel in the most desperate way.

This is the twenty-first century, in which God has called us to live for Christ in post-Christian times. To that end, we offer everything we are and everything we have for His service. If we are wise, we will recommit ourselves to expository preaching, God-centered worship, loving fellowship, pastoral care, costly discipleship, global evangelism, and practical compassion. But none of this will matter unless we recognize our need—our daily need—for the gospel. A church can only be a city on a hill if it confesses its sin and trusts in the crucifixion, resurrection, and intercession of Jesus Christ for any hope of salvation.

Notes

✝

I

THE CHURCH IN THE TWENTY-FIRST CENTURY
An Overview

1. For more on this subject, see Mark A. Noll, Nathan O. Hatch, and George R. Marsden, *The Search for Christian America* (Westchester, Ill.: Crossway, 1983).

2. Charles Colson with Ellen Santilli Vaughn, *Against the Night: Living in the New Dark Ages* (Ann Arbor, Mich.: Servant, 1989), 23–24.

3. Douglas Coupland, quoted in John Muether, "Something Short of Redemption: The Pilgrims of John Updike and Douglas Coupland," *Modern Reformation*, July/August 2001, 21.

4. Stephen Turner, "Creed," in *Up to Date* (London: Hodder & Stoughton, 1985), 138–39.

5. Robert Schuller, *Self-Love* (Old Tappan, N.J.: Revell, 1981), 24.

6. Christopher Lasch, *The Culture of Narcissism*, rev. ed. (New York: Norton, 1991), 239.

7. C. Peter Wagner, "Another New Wineskin . . . the New Apostolic Reformation," *NEXT*, Vol. 5, No. 1 (January–March 1999), 1–3.

8. Iain Murray, *Evangelicalism Divided: A Record of Crucial Change in the Years 1950 to 2000* (Edinburgh: Banner of Truth, 2000), 255.

9. James Montgomery Boice develops this argument in *Whatever Happened to the Gospel of Grace?* (Wheaton, Ill.: Crossway, 2001).

10. Notable examples include Robert Brow, "Evangelical Megashift," *Christianity Today,* 19 February 1990, 12–14; Stanley J. Grenz, *Revisioning Evangelical Theology: A Fresh Agenda for the Twenty-First Century* (Downers Grove, Ill.: InterVarsity, 1993); and Roger Olson, "The Future of Evangelical Theology," *Christianity Today,* 9 February 1998, 40–48.

11. Jerry Bridges, *The Discipline of Grace: God's Role and Our Role in the Pursuit of Holiness* (Colorado Springs: NavPress, 1994), 88.

2
MAKING GOD'S WORD PLAIN
Expository Preaching

1. Nancy Gibbs, "How Much Does the Preaching Matter?" *Time,* 17 September 2001, 55.

2. George Gaylord Simpson, quoted in Phillip E. Johnson, *Reason in the Balance: The Case Against Naturalism in Science, Law and Education* (Downers Grove, Ill.: InterVarsity, 1995), 12–13.

3. See James Montgomery Boice, *What Makes a Church Evangelical?* Today's Issues (Wheaton, Ill.: Crossway, 1999), 19–27.

4. David Brooks, *Bobos in Paradise: The New Upper Class and How They Got There* (New York: Simon & Schuster, 2000), quoted in *Modern Reformation,* January/February 2002, 36.

5. John Calvin, *Ephesians* (Edinburgh: Banner of Truth, 1973), 42.

3
GIVING PRAISE TO GOD
Corporate Worship

1. "Triumph of the Praise Songs," *Christianity Today,* 7 July 1999.

2. See Jacques Ellul, *The Humiliation of the Word,* trans. by Joyce Main Hanks (Grand Rapids: Eerdmans, 1985).

3. Leander Keck, *The Church Confident* (Nashville: Abingdon, 1993), 35.

4. R. Kent Hughes, *Disciplines of a Godly Man* (Wheaton, Ill.: Crossway, 1991), 106.

5. *Westminster Shorter Catechism,* in *The Confession of Faith* (Inverness: Publications Committee of the Free Presbyterian Church of Scotland, 1970), A. 90.

6. This principle, which comes from Johannes Oecolampadius, is discussed by Hughes Oliphant Old in *The Shaping of the Reformed Baptismal Rite in the Sixteenth Century* (Grand Rapids: Eerdmans, 1992), 119ff.

7. Martin Luther, *Luther's Works* (Philadelphia: Fortress, 1967), 54:129.

8. Ibid., 53:328.

9. Gene Edward Veith, *State of the Arts: From Bezalel to Mapplethorpe* (Wheaton, Ill.: Crossway, 1994), 202.

10. Donald Bloesch, "Whatever Happened to God?" *Christianity Today*, 5 February 2001, 54–55.

11. Marva J. Dawn, *A Royal "Waste" of Time: The Splendor of Worshiping God and Being Church for the World* (Grand Rapids: Eerdmans, 1999), 305.

12. Ibid., 64.

13. Joanne Carlson Brown, "Divine Child Abuse," *Daughters of Sarah*, Vol. 18, No. 3 (Summer, 1992), 28.

4

GROWING TOGETHER IN GROUPS
Fellowship

1. Douglas Coupland, *Generation X: Tales for an Accelerated Culture* (New York: St. Martin's, 1991), 30.

2. Ibid., 69.

3. Ibid., 171.

4. Ibid., 183.

5. Charles Colson and Ellen Santilli Vaughn, *The Body* (Dallas: Word, 1992), 32.

6. Laurent Belsie, "Ethnic Diversity Grows, but not Integration," *The Christian Science Monitor*, 14 March 2001.

7. Ray C. Stedman, *Body Life* (Glendale, Calif.: Regal, 1972), 39.

8. Christopher Lasch, *The Culture of Narcissism*, rev. ed. (New York: Norton, 1991), 242.

9. Charles Reich, *The Greening of America: The Coming of a New Consciousness and the Rebirth of a Future* (New York: Bantam, 1971), 7.

10. Helen Fielding, *Bridget Jones: The Edge of Reason* (New York: Penguin, 2001).

5

SHEPHERDING GOD'S FLOCK
Pastoral Care

1. Leon Morris, *The Apostolic Preaching of the Cross*, 3d ed. (Grand Rapids: Eerdmans, 1965), 11–27.

2. Alan Wolfe, *Moral Freedom*, quoted in Fareed Zakaria, "The Character of our Campuses," *Newsweek*, 28 May 2001, 31.

6

THINKING AND ACTING BIBLICALLY
Discipleship

1. Dietrich Bonhoeffer, *The Cost of Discipleship* (New York: Macmillan, 1963), 99.

2. Jonathan Edwards, *The Works of Jonathan Edwards*, 2 vols. (1834; repr. Edinburgh: Banner of Truth, 1974), I:xxv.

3. Marva J. Dawn, *Reaching Out without Dumbing Down* (Grand Rapids: Eerdmans, 1995), 114.

4. Iain H. Murray, *Evangelicalism Divided: A Record of Crucial Change in the Years 1950 to 2000* (Edinburgh: Banner of Truth, 2000), 255.

5. Douglas D. Webster, *Selling Jesus: What's Wrong with Marketing the Church* (Downers Grove, Ill.: InterVarsity, 1992), 20.

6. Christopher Lasch, *The Culture of Narcissism: American Life in an Age of Diminishing Expectations* (New York: Norton, 1991), 239.

7. David Wells, *No Place for Truth, or, Whatever Happened to Evangelical Theology?* (Grand Rapids: Eerdmans, 1993), 182.

8. Ibid., 179.

9. James M. Boice, *Mind Renewal in a Mindless Age* (Grand Rapids: Baker, 1993).

7

REACHING THE WORLD
Missions and Evangelism

1. Tom and Cynthia Hale, "Disciples Needed for the Twenty-First Century," unpublished letter (used by permission).

2. See David Barrett's annual report on the "Status of Global Mission" in the January issue of the *International Bulletin of Missionary Research.*

3. Ralph Winter, "Unreached Peoples: Recent Developments in the Concept," *Mission Frontiers*, August/September 1989, 12.

4. John Piper discusses many of these passages in *Let the Nations Be Glad! The Supremacy of God in Missions* (Grand Rapids: Baker, 1993), 172–205.

5. Andrew F. Walls, *The Missionary Movement in Christian History: Studies in the Transmission of Faith* (Maryknoll, N.Y.: Orbis, 1996), 51.

6. For some helpful ideas on doing this, see John Lindner, "A Different Kind of Missionary," *World Christian*, September, 2002, 20–24; Jonathan J. Bonk, *Missions and Money: Affluence as a Western Missionary Problem*, American Society of Missiology Series, No. 15 (Maryknoll, N.Y.: Orbis, 1991).

7. George R. Hunsberger, "Sizing Up the Shape of the Church," in *The Church Between Gospel and Culture: The Emerging Mission in North America*, ed. by George R. Hunsberger and Craig Van Gelder (Grand Rapids: Eerdmans, 1996), 333–46.

8
SERVING WITH COMPASSION
Mercy Ministry

1. Pierce Pettis, "When I Grow Up," Tinsletown (1988). Used by permission of the author.

2. William H. Willimon and Thomas H. Naylor, *The Abandoned Generation: Rethinking Higher Education* (Grand Rapids: Eerdmans, 1995), 38–39.

3. See Matthew 11:11; 12:48–50; 18:3–6, 10–14; 28:10.

4. Timothy J. Keller, *Ministries of Mercy: The Call of the Jericho Road* (Grand Rapids: Zondervan, 1989), 80, 83.

5. Marvin N. Olasky, *The Tragedy of American Compassion* (Wheaton, Ill.: Crossway, 1992).

6. Mark Greene, The London Institute for Contemporary Christianity (used by permission).

9
WHY THE CHURCH NEEDS THE GOSPEL
Repentance and Renewal

1. Quoted in Damon Linker, "Radical Niceness," *National Review*, 28 May 2001, 61.

2. *Liberated Bridegroom*, quoted in Christopher Lasch, *The Culture of Narcissism: American Life in an Age of Diminishing Expectations* (New York: Norton, 1991), 187.

3. Stanley Hauerwas and William H. Willimon, *Resident Aliens* (Nashville: Abingdon, 1989), 46–47.

4. Quoted in Os Guinness, *Dining with the Devil: The Megachurch Movement Flirts with Modernity* (Grand Rapids: Baker, 1993), 59.

5. Personal correspondence (used by permission).

6. Mark A. Noll, *Seasons of Grace* (Grand Rapids: Baker, 1997), 52–53. Used by permission.

ACTION GUIDE

for Pastors and Other Church Leaders

by Jonathan David Olsen

This Action Guide is designed to help pastors, elders, and other church leaders take their ministry to the next level. The *Evaluating Your Ministry* section is a guide to help you look at your ministry in a biblically critical way. The *Practical Recommendations* section provides some tangible ways to help your ministry grow and make it more thoroughly biblical. The *Helpful Resources* section gives an introductory bibliography of reference tools and resources for those involved with the ministry of your church. Our hope and prayer is that God will use the Action Guide as a tool for leaders' self-evaluation and further growth, either in a particular area of ministry or for the whole church.

CHAPTER 1: A CHURCH FOR THE TWENTY-FIRST CENTURY

EVALUATING YOUR MINISTRY

1. Name some ways you see post-Christian thought influencing the members of your church. In what specific ways do you see them acting out of self-love rather than out of love for Christ?

2. What are the ramifications for your ministry if truth is considered relative and Christianity only relatively true?

3. What is your church's mission statement? How well can your leaders repeat it? Your members? How do you communicate the vision?

4. In what ways are you teaching your church that everything else depends upon the plain teaching of God's Word (even if your congregation has a high view of Scripture)?

5. What does your congregation believe about the importance of church membership? What signs do you see of their commitment to the body of Christ, to living and being the church? Where do you see a lack of commitment?

6. What is your church's philosophy of and strategy for evangelism? How well do your members understand that evangelism is not so much a special event as it is a part of their everyday living? How are they sharing their faith?

Practical Recommendations

1. Pray that God will keep you and all those who teach in your church faithful to His Word in every area of ministry.

2. Ask the elders and other church leaders to pray for and carefully listen to your preaching and teaching. Ask them to evaluate how faithfully you are teaching the Bible and applying it to the areas of the congregation's need.

3. Call the elders and staff of your church together to reconsider your mission statement. Develop a statement if you do not have one, possibly including some of the ideas from this book. Make sure you can show how every aspect of your vision is Word-based, Christ-centered, and God-glorifying.

4. Study Acts 2:42–47. With your elders and staff, develop a plan for including the elements of the early church's fellowship (Bible reading, prayer, etc.) in all of your church meetings throughout the week.

5. Alert the youth of your church to the dangers of narcissism and relativism. Help them think through the implications that these contemporary trends have for their spiritual lives. Offer a biblical response and alternative.

Helpful Resources

Armstrong, John, ed. *The Coming Evangelical Crisis: Current Challenges to the Authority of the Scripture and the Gospel.* Chicago: Moody, 1997.

Boice, James M., and Benjamin Sasse, eds. *Here We Stand: A Call From Confessing Evangelicals.* Grand Rapids: Baker, 1996.

Boice, James M. *Whatever Happened to the Gospel of Grace?* Wheaton, Ill.: Crossway, 2001.

Dever, Mark. *Nine Marks of a Healthy Church.* Wheaton, Ill.: Crossway, 2000.

Frame, John. *No Other God: A Response to Open Theism.* Phillipsburg, N.J.: P & R, 2001.

Horton, Michael, ed. *Power Religion: The Selling Out of the Evangelical Church.* Chicago: Moody, 1992.

Ryken, Philip. *Is Jesus the Only Way?* Wheaton, Ill.: Crossway, 1999.

Sproul, R. C. *Getting the Gospel Right: The Tie that Binds Evangelicals Together.* Grand Rapids: Baker, 1999.

_____. *Knowing Scripture.* Downers Grove, Ill.: InterVarsity, 1977.

Ware, Bruce. *God's Lesser Glory: The Diminished God of Open Theism.* Wheaton, Ill.: Crossway, 2000.

Wells, David. *No Place For Truth: Or Whatever Happened to Evangelical Theology?* Grand Rapids: Eerdmans, 1993.

CHAPTER 2: MAKING GOD'S WORD PLAIN

EVALUATING YOUR MINISTRY

1. What are the goals of your preaching ministry? How effectively are you meeting them?

2. What does your weekly schedule reveal about the priority you place on preaching and preparing to preach? Do other pastoral duties revolve around preaching, or does preaching get squeezed in around them?

3. Go back over your sermon texts and titles for the past year or so. What have you been preaching, and why? How well are you covering Scripture? Theology? Practical Christian discipleship?

4. What indications are there that your congregation has a clear grasp of key biblical doctrines? How effectively in your preaching are you exposing your congregation to the "big picture" of God's redemptive work? Are you giving them the whole counsel of God?

5. Consider some of your recent sermons. How much of your content comes directly from teaching a biblical text, and how much from outside? Is the content of your sermon guarded and guided by the larger context of your particular passage?

6. Consider your illustrations. How often do you look to the Scriptures in order to illustrate your point? Are your illustrations for the universal church as well as for the personal needs of your congregation?

7. Evaluate your application of biblical doctrine. To what extent are practical applications actually coming from the biblical text being prepared?

Practical Recommendations

1. Block out certain hours each week that are designated as uninterrupted time for sermon preparation—earlier in the week is usually better.

2. If you are just starting to preach expositional sermons, it may be helpful to begin with a small epistle such as Ephesians or Philippians, or with Mark, the shortest gospel.

3. Begin talking with other ministers who do expository preaching. Ask them for constructive criticism about your preaching, with the goal of becoming both faithful to the biblical text and relevant to contemporary culture.

4. Get one good expositional commentary or sermon series and study how the material is constructed. (InterVarsity's Bible Speaks Today series, Crossway's Preaching the Word series, and any of Baker's expositional commentaries by James M. Boice are all good places to start.)

5. Set up a local ministers' fellowship or preaching society. Meet on a regular basis in order to discuss preaching and to critique sermons.

Helpful Resources

Begg, Alistair. *Preaching for God's Glory.* Wheaton, Ill.: Crossway, 1999.

Chapell, Bryan. *Christ-Centered Preaching: Redeeming the Expository Sermon.* Grand Rapids: Baker, 1994.

Clowney, Edmund. *Preaching and Biblical Theology.* Phillipsburg, N.J.: P & R, 2002.

_____. *The Unfolding Mystery: Discovering Christ in the Old Testament.* Colorado Springs, Colo.: NavPress, 1988.

Workshop on Biblical Preaching. This annual preaching conference is held in May at College Church in Wheaton, Ill. Contact College Church at (630) 668-0878.

Greidanus, Sidney. *Preaching Christ from the Old Testament: A Contemporary Hermeneutical Method.* Grand Rapids: Eerdmans, 1999.

Kistler, Don, ed. *Feed My Sheep! A Passionate Plea for Preaching.* Morgan, Pa.: Soli Deo Gloria, 2002.

MacArthur, John. *Rediscovering Expository Preaching.* Dallas: Word, 1992.

Martin, Albert. *What's Wrong with Preaching Today?* London: Banner of Truth, 1967.

Old, Hughes Oliphant. *The Reading and Preaching of the Scriptures in the Worship of the Christian Church* (7 vols). Grand Rapids: Eerdmans, 1998–.

Piper, John. *The Supremacy of God in Preaching.* Grand Rapids: Baker, 1990.

Stott, John. *Between Two Worlds: The Art of Preaching in the Twentieth Century.* Grand Rapids: Eerdmans, 1982.

Trimp, C. *Preaching and the History of Salvation: Continuing an Unfinished Discussion.* Dyer, Ind.: Nelson D. Kloosterman, 1996. Contact Mid-America Reformed Seminary for copies: 229 Seminary Drive, Dyer, IN 46311.

Vines, Jerry, and Jim Shaddix. *Power in the Pulpit: How to Prepare and Deliver Expository Sermons.* Chicago: Moody, 1999.

CHAPTER 3: GIVE PRAISE TO GOD

EVALUATING YOUR MINISTRY

1. Ask the members of your congregation two questions: What is worship? Who do you think the primary audience is/should be in worship? How well do their answers agree with your church's theology of worship?

2. Review your order of worship. In what ways does it advance the ultimate human goal of glorifying God and enjoying Him forever?

3. Chart out the amount of time that is spent on each element in your worship service. What does this reflect about your priorities regarding corporate worship?

4. Evaluate and discuss what is taught in your worship music. Does the content reflect man-centered or God-centered worship? To what extent does your music communicate the truths of the Christian faith? How well do the psalms, hymns, and spiritual songs connect with the other elements of your worship service?

5. How do your people prepare for Sunday worship? How are children taught to prepare for and participate in corporate worship?

Practical Recommendations

1. Take your weekly bulletin and compare it with the standard elements of worship found in Scripture. Determine what needs to be added or altered to make your worship services more fully biblical.

2. Develop a biblical theology of worship. Include everyone who has any kind of leading role in worship in the discussion. Together with the elders of your church, evaluate what changes might need to be made in light of Scripture.

3. Begin to conduct regular meetings with everyone involved in leading worship in your church. Constantly analyze and reevaluate the faithfulness, reverence, and teaching of your corporate worship experience.

4. Conduct basic training in the biblical theology of worship for your ministers and for others who help lead worship.

Helpful Resources

Boice, James and Paul Jones. *Hymns for a Modern Reformation*. Philadelphia: Tenth Music, 2001. Contact the Alliance of Confessing Evangelicals at (215) 546-3696 or www.alliancenet.org.

Dawn, Marva. *Reaching Out Without Dumbing Down: A Theology of Worship for the Turn-of-the-Century Culture*. Grand Rapids: Eerdmans, 1995.

Duncan, J. Ligon, Philip Ryken, and Derek Thomas, eds. *Give Praise to God: Sola Scriptura et Soli Deo Gloria: Essays in Honor of James Montgomery Boice*. Phillipsburg, N.J.: P & R (forthcoming).

Godfrey, Robert. *Pleasing God in Our Worship*. Wheaton, Ill.: Crossway, 1999.

Horton, Michael. *A Better Way: Rediscovering the Drama of God-Centered Worship*. Grand Rapids: Baker, 2002.

Hustad, Donald. *True Worship: Reclaiming the Wonder and Majesty*. Wheaton, Ill.: Shaw, 1998.

Johanssen, Calvin. *Discipling Music Ministry: Twenty-first Century Directions*. Peabody, Mass.: Hendrickson, 1992.

Old, Hughes Oliphant. *Worship That Is Reformed According to Scripture*, Guides to the Reformed Tradition. Atlanta: John Knox, 1984.

_____. *Leading in Prayer: A Workbook for Worship.* Grand Rapids: Eerdmans, 1995.

Philadelphia Conference on Reformation Theology: *Worship* (1999). For conference tapes contact the Alliance of Confessing Evangelicals at (215) 546-3696 or www.alliancenet.org.

Wilson-Dickson, Andrew. *The Story of Christian Music: From Gregorian Chant to Black Gospel: An Illustrated Guide to All the Major Traditions of Music in Worship.* Minneapolis, Minn.: Augsburg Fortress, 1997.

CHAPTER 4: GROWING TOGETHER IN SMALL GROUPS

EVALUATING YOUR MINISTRY

1. How many people in your church are in a small group? Which segments of your congregation are least likely to be involved in one?

2. What kind of small group Bible studies does your church have? How many are evangelistic? Inductive? Directed? Topical?

3. How do you invite and encourage new people in your church to participate in small groups? How do new members get plugged in?

4. What differences are small groups making in the lives of church members? How are people growing in their knowledge of Scripture, their service to God, and their love for one another?

5. How does your church identify, train, support, and oversee those who lead small groups?

6. What active steps does your church take in training small group leaders to meet the spiritual and practical needs of the members of their group?

Practical Recommendations

1. Develop, in writing, the purpose and philosophy of small group ministry in your church. Articulate how every element of small group ministry is Word-centered in order to be God-glorifying.

2. Allocate regular time for a staff member or church officer to focus on leader recruitment and development in your small group ministry.

3. Host an annual small group seminar to train people how to teach the Bible and give spiritual care in a small group setting.

4. Appoint a biblically qualified person to visit and oversee the work of each small group.

5. Develop a plan for getting new members involved in a small group.

Helpful Resources

Arnold, Jeff. *Small Group Starter Kit: 6 Studies for New Groups.* Downers Grove, Ill.: InterVarsity, 1995.

Bonhoeffer, Dietrich. *Life Together: A Discussion of Christian Fellowship.* San Francisco: HarperCollins, 1978.

Jacks, Bob, Betty Jacks and Ron Wormser. *Your Home a Lighthouse.* Colorado Springs: NavPress, 1987.

Nyquist, James. *Leading Bible Discussions.* Downers Grove, Ill.: InterVarsity, 1985.

Ryken, Philip. *The Communion of Saints: Living in Fellowship with the People of God.* Phillipsburg, N.J.: P & R, 2001. (A Spiritual Gifts Inventory is included as an appendix.)

Redeemer Presbyterian Church. *Turbo Group Material.* Redeemer Church has material for training potential small group leaders. The material includes the purpose and hands-on methodology for small groups with studies in Acts 2 and 2 Timothy. Contact Redeemer at (212) 808-4460 or www.redeemer.com.

Wilhoit, Jim and Leland Ryken. *Effective Bible Teaching.* Grand Rapids: Baker, 1988.

Wray, Daniel. *The Importance of the Local Church.* Edinburgh: Banner of Truth, 1991.

CHAPTER 5: SHEPHERDING GOD'S FLOCK

EVALUATING YOUR MINISTRY

1. What is the overall plan for the pastoral care of your church? How does this plan include the pastors, elders, and other congregational leaders?

2. How much of your ministry time is devoted to meeting with people? Are most of the meetings you have with people in the church initiated by them or by you? Why?

3. What are the main demographic groups in your church? How are the pastors and elders prepared to meet their particular needs? Which groups or individuals are most likely to get overlooked or neglected for pastoral care?

4. How much pastoral care do you delegate to others? How do you support those who are helping to provide pastoral care?

5. How does your church leadership learn about the needs of your congregation? How do you and other leaders go about praying for and meeting these needs?

6. How well are you aware of members' absences from the church? How long does it take before someone is missed? How does the church respond?

7. What is your pastoral response to prevalent sin patterns or scandalous sin within your congregation? How effectively does your leadership deal with cases that require church discipline?

Practical Recommendations

1. Assess and pray for the spiritual health of your fellow leaders.

2. Take time to "shepherd the shepherds." Spend regular time discipling and encouraging those who are leading the rest of the flock.

3. Have the leaders of your church go through the list of members in prayer. Consider how each member is doing spiritually. For any whose present spiritual condition is unknown, develop a plan for finding out how they are doing and then addressing their spiritual needs.

4. Conduct pastoral training sessions on a regular basis. Develop a training program for new or potential elders. Conduct an annual retreat to work on pastoral skills with your current leaders.

5. Identify the people in your church who are most likely to "fall through the cracks." Develop a realistic yet comprehensive plan for ministering to them.

6. Conduct "exit interviews" with those who are leaving your church. Ask them to evaluate and make recommendations for your pastoral care-giving.

Helpful Resources

Adams, Jay. *Shepherding God's Flock: A Handbook on Pastoral Ministry, Counseling, and Leadership.* Grand Rapids: Zondervan, 1974.

Armstrong, John. *The Compromised Church: The Present Evangelical Crisis.* Wheaton, Ill.: Crossway, 1998. (Especially note Al Mohler's chapter on Discipline.)

Baxter, Richard. *The Reformed Pastor.* Edinburgh: Banner of Truth, 1994.

Berghoef, Gerard and Lester DeKoster, eds. *The Elders Handbook: A Practical Guide For Church Leaders.* Grand Rapids: Christian Library, 1979.

Bridges, Charles. *The Christian Ministry.* London: Banner of Truth, 1976.

MacArthur, John. *Rediscovering Pastoral Ministry: Shaping Contemporary Ministry with Biblical Mandates.* Dallas: Word, 1995.

McCartney, Dan. *Why Does It Have To Hurt?: The Meaning of Christian Suffering.* Phillipsburg, N.J.: P & R, 1998.

Sande, Ken. *The Peacemakers: A Biblical Guide to Resolving Personal Conflict.* Grand Rapids: Baker, 1991.

Strauch, Alexander. *Biblical Eldership: An Urgent Call to Restore Biblical Church Leadership.* Littleton, Colo.: Lewis & Roth, 1995.

Witmer, Timothy. *Shepherd Our Sheep* (SOS) workshop material. To order materials contact Timothy Witmer at (215) 572-3831 or twitmer@wts.edu.

CHAPTER 6: THINKING AND ACTING BIBLICALLY

EVALUATING YOUR MINISTRY

1. What is your church's overall vision for its discipleship ministry? What kind of hearts, minds, and wills are you seeking to grow? How does this vision fit into the overall work of your church's ministry? How is discipleship integrated into the life of your congregation?

2. What are your congregation's greatest obstacles to true Christian discipleship?

3. How do elders and other leaders learn to disciple people for Christ? How much of their time is spent running church programs, and how much is devoted to personal ministry?

4. How does your church disciple people of various ages? What groups or individuals in your congregation tend to get overlooked for intentional discipleship?

5. How is God's Word used as a means of discipleship? Are there areas of ministry that lack a biblical focus?

6. How does your congregation learn to make the connection between Christian *thinking* and Christian *living?*

Practical Recommendations

1. Gather the church leadership to develop a "master plan of discipleship" for the congregation. Write down your intentions for meeting the discipleship needs of everyone in the church, from infants to the elderly. Be sure not to

overlook the vital task of training parents how to disciple their children.

2. Encourage staff, elders, and other church leaders to spend more time talking with people about the Bible. Challenge your members with questions about what sacrifices they are making for Christ and how they are renewing their minds.

3. Meet with the leaders of your small groups to ensure they are not providing a "spiritual self-help program," but offering sound teaching from the Bible.

4. Consider holding an annual conference that helps Christians interact with culture. Topics could range from Christianity and the Arts or Christianity and the Environment to the Church and the State.

5. Have a gifted and willing person appointed as a Bible school/discipleship coordinator. This person should oversee the Sunday school curriculum as well as any material used for personal discipleship.

6. Pray regularly for the Holy Spirit to bless the ministry of God's Word. Pray for the discipleship needs of the congregation not only in private, but also during corporate worship.

Helpful Resources

Boice, James. *Christ's Call to Discipleship.* Chicago: Moody, 1986.

―――. *Renewing Your Mind in a Mindless Age: Learning to Think & Act Biblically.* Grand Rapids: Kregel, 2001.

Bonhoeffer, Dietrich. *The Cost of Discipleship.* New York: Macmillan, 1963.

Coleman, Robert. *The Master Plan of Discipleship.* Old Tappan, N.J.: Revell, 1987.

Colson, Charles. *How Now Shall We Live?* Wheaton, Ill.: Tyndale, 1999.

Eims, Leroy. *The Lost Art of Disciple Making.* Grand Rapids: Zondervan, 1978.

Ferguson, Sinclair. *The Christian Life: A Doctrinal Introduction.* Edinburgh: Banner of Truth, 1981.

Packer, James. *Knowing God.* Downers Grove, Ill.: InterVarsity, 1973.

Ryken, Leland. *Culture in Christian Perspective: A Door to Understanding & Enjoying the Arts.* Portland, Oreg.: Multnomah, 1986.

CHAPTER 7: MISSION TO THE WORLD

EVALUATING YOUR MINISTRY

1. How is your congregation exposed to missions in general, and specifically, to individual missionaries and the work they are doing?

2. In what ways is your congregation involved in missions— prayer, financial support, short-term projects, visiting/ hosting missionaries? Which areas of involvement seem underdeveloped?

3. What proportion of your church's overall giving goes to the work of missions? Of the money that is given, what is the breakdown: overseas missions church planting, denominational giving, or specific ministries funded by the church? Do the figures reflect your intended missions priorities?

4. Do your missionaries receive adequate prayer support? How often are they prayed for in corporate worship or small group settings? Do your prayers reflect the global concerns of the church, including the persecuted church?

5. What is your track record for sending out missionaries from your congregation? How are potential short- or long-term missionaries identified, trained, and encouraged?

6. How does missions fit into the overall application of "lifestyle evangelism" for the members of your congregation? How are missionaries and the work of missions incorporated into your children's program?

7. To what extent are the members of your church engaging in personal evangelism? How are they equipped and encouraged to share their faith? How many church members have witnessed in the last week? The last month? The last year?

8. How many members join your church as new converts each year? In what targeted evangelism (people / groups) is your church intentionally engaged? What local communities are being overlooked for gospel outreach?

Practical Recommendations

1. Develop and articulate a clear and intentional philosophy of missions and church planting, as well as a strategy to accomplish your stated goals.

2. Put together a written quiz for your congregation. Test them on the basic information about your missions program as well as the overall mission of Christ's church.

3. Involve church members in a missions commission that has clear leadership and definite goals.

4. Conduct short-term mission trips. Involve church leaders as a catalyst for congregational involvement.

5. Host an annual missions conference. Invite outside speakers, including both missionaries you support and international Christian leaders.

6. Make every effort to identify and minister to minority groups and internationals near your church.

7. Develop an effective strategy for communicating missionary needs to your membership. Set up regular prayer meetings for missions, church planting, and evangelism.

Helpful Resources

Allen, Roland. *The Spontaneous Expansion of the Church: And the Causes that Hinder It.* Eugene, Oreg.: Wipf & Stock, 1997.

Coleman, Robert. *The Master Plan of Evangelism.* Old Tappan, N.J.: Revell, 1987.

Johnstone, Patrick. *Operation World: When We Pray God Works.* Waynesboro, Ga.: Paternoster, 2001.

Evangelism Explosion Starter Kit. Produced by James D. Kennedy from Coral Ridge Presbyterian Church in Fort Lauderdale, Fla. Contact them at (954) 491-6100 or www.eeinternational.org.

Evangelical Missions Quarterly. A quarterly publication by the Evangelism and Missions Information Service of the Billy Graham Center at Wheaton College. Contact EMIS at (630) 752-7168 or www.wheaton.edu/bgc/emis.

Kuiper, Rienk B. *God-Centered Evangelism: A Presentation of the Scriptural Theology of Evangelism.* Grand Rapids: Baker, 1961.

McDowell, Bruce, and Anees Zaka. *Muslims and Christians at the Table.* Phillipsburg, N.J.: P & R, 1999.

Miller, C. John. *Powerful Evangelism for the Powerless.* Phillipsburg, N.J.: P & R, 1997.

Packer, James. *Evangelism and the Sovereignty of God.* Downers Grove, Ill.: InterVarsity, 1961.

Piper, John. *Let the Nations Be Glad: The Supremacy of God in Missions.* Grand Rapids: Baker, 1993.

Van Engen, Charles. *God's Missionary People: Rethinking the Purpose of the Local Church.* Grand Rapids: Baker, 1991.

Winter, Ralph. *Perspectives on the World Christian Movement: A Reader.* Waynesboro, Ga.: William Carey Library, 1992.

CHAPTER 8: ACTIVE COMPASSION THROUGH SERVICE

EVALUATING YOUR MINISTRY

1. How does the socio-economic make-up of your congregation compare with the surrounding community? What does this comparison reveal about your past ministry priorities and present ministry opportunities?

2. What are the main vehicles for mercy ministry in and near your church? What are the significant areas of need in the community for which your church presently has no outreach?

3. List the various ways that individuals in your church are personally involved in community outreach. What percentage of your membership has significant involvement in mercy ministry inside or outside your church?

4. Look at Matthew 25:31–46. How well does your church follow our Lord's description of mercy ministry? What aspects of mercy are missing?

5. What initial and ongoing training do you provide for diaconal and mercy ministries?

6. What role does teaching God's Word have in your mercy ministries? Is there a biblical balance between Word and deed?

Practical Recommendations

1. Here is a possible pathway for setting up new mercy ministries: (a) identify the real needs in and around your church; (b) begin to pray; (c) gather those who are willing and gifted to meet the needs; (d) research and arrange logistics by developing a list of assets and capacities in the neighborhood and the church.

2. Meet with other churches that are close to you and find out what they are doing in the area of mercy ministry. Find ways to join them in what they are doing and seek to meet further needs that are not being met.

3. Develop pastoral contact with churches from various ethnic groups. Seek opportunities to partner in ministry.

4. Identify people in your congregation with relevant expertise and seek to deploy them for the work of mercy ministry. Develop a plan for identifying and equipping new leaders.

5. Provide ongoing training for diaconal ministries of mercy by giving those who are gifted and willing the opportunities to serve in the context of mercy ministry.

6. Develop and oversee a well-thought-out benevolence policy for the deacons to use as they meet practical needs.

Helpful Resources

Barnett, James. *The Diaconate: A Full and Equal Order.* Valley Forge, Pa.: Trinity Press International, 1995.

Berghoef, Gerard and Lester DeKoster, eds. *The Deacons Handbook: A Manual of Stewardship.* Grand Rapids: Christian Library, 1980.

Conn, Harvie and Manuel Ortiz. *Urban Ministry: The Kingdom, the City and the People of God.* Downers Grove, Ill.: InterVarsity, 2001.

Keller, Timothy. *Ministries of Mercy: The Call of the Jericho Road.* Phillipsburg, N.J.: P & R, 1997.

McGee, Elsie. *Diakonia in the Classical Reformed Tradition and Today.* Grand Rapids: Eerdmans, 1989.

Sherman, Amy. *Restorers of Hope: Reaching the Poor in Your Community with Church-Based Ministries that Work.* Wheaton, Ill.: Crossway, 1997.

Sider, Ronald, Philip Olson, and Heidi Unruh. *Churches That Make a Difference.* Grand Rapids: Baker, 2002.

Strauch, Alexander. *The New Testament Deacon: The Church's Minister of Mercy.* Littleton, Colo.: Lewis & Roth, 1992.

Van Klinken, Jaap. *Diakonia.* Grand Rapids: Eerdmans, 1989.

CHAPTER 9: WHY THE CHURCH NEEDS THE GOSPEL

EVALUATING YOUR MINISTRY

1. How are the implications of the Gospel for everyday living communicated in the ministry of your church? What role does the Gospel play in the daily Christian experiences of your church leaders?

2. How is the remedy for sin presented in your preaching and teaching of the Gospel? How do you equip your congregation to explain the biblical Gospel of God's grace as the answer to the world's real problems?

3. How do you and the leaders of your church encourage the congregation to pray for the universal church, especially pastors and other Christian leaders? How often does your church pray corporately for the holiness of the universal church?

4. How does your leadership encourage the congregation to confess sin? Do you have a specified time in your worship service for confession, either private or corporate? Is there time for confession in small groups and other ministry settings?

Practical Recommendations

1. Prepare a survey for your church. Ask members to define the Gospel and to describe its importance for everyday living.

2. Spend regular time with other leaders to pray for holiness and joy in the Gospel. Allow this to overflow into the life of the congregation during corporate prayers.

3. Teach church leaders, as well as the congregation, to be intentional in their prayers. Praise God for His holiness, while at the same time confessing ways that you continually fall short of that holiness. Pray for the sanctifying effects of the Cross to be evident in the life of your church.

4. Remind your congregation as often as you can that Jesus Christ and His Gospel will always be the ultimate answer to their every need.

Helpful Resources

Boice, James. *Whatever Happened to the Gospel of Grace?* Wheaton, Ill.: Crossway, 2001.

Bridges, Jerry. *The Discipline of Grace: God's Role and Our Role in the Pursuit of Holiness.* Colorado Springs: NavPress, 1994.

Chapell, Bryan. *Holiness by Grace: Delighting in the Joy That Is Our Strength.* Wheaton, Ill.: Crossway, 2001.

Horton, Michael. *Putting Amazing Back into Grace.* Grand Rapids: Baker, 1994.

Lovelace, Richard. *Dynamics of Spiritual Life.* Downers Grove, Ill.: InterVarsity, 1979.

Luther, Martin. *Christian Liberty.* Philadelphia: Fortress, 1957.

Piper, John. *Desiring God: Meditations of a Christian Hedonist.* Sisters, Oreg.: Multnomah, 1996.

Sproul, R. C. *Getting the Gospel Right: The Tie That Binds Evangelicals Together.* Grand Rapids: Baker, 1999.

_____. *Faith Alone: The Evangelical Doctrine of Justification.* Grand Rapids: Baker, 1995.

CITY ON A HILL TEAM

ACQUIRING EDITOR:
Greg Thornton

COPY EDITOR:
Cheryl Dunlop

BACK COVER COPY:
Wendy Peterson

COVER DESIGN:
Lecy Design

INTERIOR DESIGN:
Ragont Design

PRINTING AND BINDING:
Dickinson Press Inc.

The typeface for the text of this book is
Centaur MT